The U.S. Invasion of Panama

The Truth Behind Operation 'Just Cause'

The U.S. Invasion of Panama

The Truth Behind Operation 'Just Cause'

Prepared by the
Independent Commission of Inquiry on the
U.S. Invasion of Panama

South End Press   **Boston**

Cover design by Cynthia Peters
The cover photo, taken by an unknown Panamanian, is a picture of
the El Chorrillo neighborhood after it was bombed during the invasion.
Text design and production by Dee Stapp
Printed in the U.S.A.
Second edition, first printing

Library of Congress Cataloging-in-Publication Data

The U.S. invasion of Panama : The truth behind Operation 'Just Cause'
/ prepared by the Independent Commission of Inquiry on the U.S.
Invasion of Panama.
   p.   cm.
   ISBN 0-89608-408-6 : $25.00. -- ISBN 0-89608-407-8 (pbk.) : $10.00
1. Panama--History--American invasion, 1989.   I. Independent
Commission of Inquiry on the U.S. Invasion of Panama. II. Title: US
invasion of Panama.
F1567.U2 1991
972.8705'3--dc20   90-23120
                                        CIP

South End Press, 116 Saint Botolph Street, Boston, MA 02115

98 97 96 95 94 93 92   1 2 3 4 5 6 7 8 9

Table of Contents

Acknowledgments

The work of the Commission of Inquiry has been made possible first and foremost by the brave women and men in Panama who, at substantial risk to themselves, helped in the gathering of this information. Some are mentioned by name in this book; others could not be identified for obvious reasons. All have earned our profound respect and thanks.

We also would like to give special thanks to Lucille Banta, Robert Boehm, Ben Chaney, Georgia Clark, The Funding Exchange, Howard Gressey, Deirdre Griswold, Beth Lamont, Corliss Lamont, Mojalefa Ralekhetho, Jim Ricks, Larry Schilling, Eduardo Suárez, Rosa de la Torre and Angela Vera for their assistance.

The members of the Commission are:

Kathy Andrade, V. Rex Archibold, Esmeralda Brown, Humberto R. Brown, Ramsey Clark, Ben Dupuy, Francois Felix, Graham Greene, Robert Knight, Paul B. Martin, Eli C. Messinger, Jelayne Miles, Paul O'Dwyer, George Priestley, Michael Ratner, Ellen Ray, Carlos E. Russell, William H. Schaap, Bob Schwartz, Leonardo Sidnez, Waldaba Stewart, Roderick Thurton, Valerie Van Isler, George Vickers, Lucius Walker and Dale Wiehoff.

Commission Staff: Gavrielle Gemma and Teresa Gutierrez (Project Directors), Milsa Barrow, Brian Becker, Carl Glenn and Osmán Morales-Roca (researcher). Carl Glenn provided the translations of speeches and interviews.

Independent Commission of Inquiry on
    the U.S. Invasion of Panama
36 East 12th Street, 6th floor
New York, N.Y. 10003

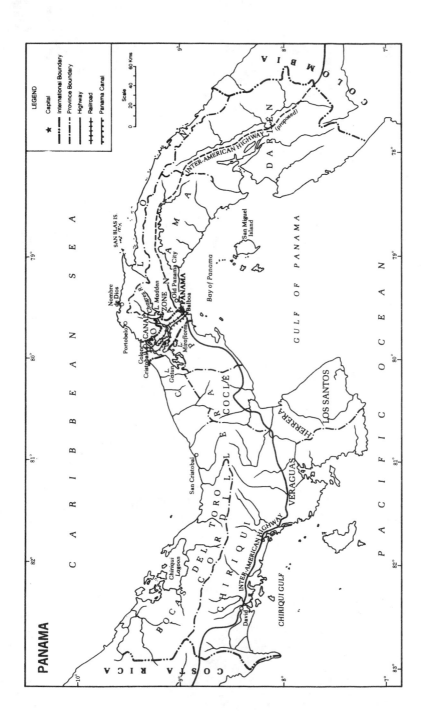

PANAMA

LEGEND

★ Capital
International Boundary
Province Boundary
Highway
Railroad
Panama Canal

Scale
0 20 40 60 Kms

CARIBBEAN SEA

COSTA RICA

COLOMBIA

PACIFIC OCEAN

GULF OF PANAMA

Bay of Panama

BOCAS DEL TORO

CHIRIQUI

VERAGUAS

HERRERA

LOS SANTOS

COCLÉ

COLÓN

PANAMA

DARIEN

CANAL ZONE

SAN BLAS IS.

San Miguel Island

Nombre de Dios

Portobelo

Colón

Cristóbal

L. Gatun

Madden

Chagres R.

Miraflores

Balboa

PANAMA

Old Panama City

San Cristobal

Chiriqui Lagoon

CHIRIQUI GULF

David

INTER-AMERICAN HIGHWAY

INTER-AMERICAN HIGHWAY (proposed)

Introduction

When this book reaches the public, it will be one year since the brutal and racist U.S. invasion of Panama. One year since a full-scale military operation involving 24,000 troops with high-tech weaponry created terror in the middle of the night, and for weeks after, in every city and rural area of Panama. As the Report of the Commission shows, from 1,000 to 4,000 Panamanians were killed, thousands more were wounded, and more than 20,000 found themselves homeless.[1]

Thousands more Panamanians were arrested, including union leaders, university professors, political organizers, government officials, journalists and military personnel. Some were held for weeks; some are still incarcerated. All those arrested had one thing in common. Each was known to be a defender of Panamanian independence and sovereignty and opposed to the U.S. invasion.

Once again the executive branch of the U.S. government, headed by the President, had taken upon itself to launch a war not authorized by Congress. Once again, Congress allowed it. To this day, there has been not one hearing or Congressional investigation into this monstrous event, even though it violated numerous international treaties and agreements, the U.S. Constitution, and the sovereignty and independence of Panama.

Congress, with few exceptions, was a cheering squad for the invasion. The media, every television station, every major newspaper participated in a virtual orgy of applause while covering up what was really taking place in Panama. One less experienced anchorman attempting an analysis was summarily shut up while on the air.

It seemed no one was getting the facts, and no one in the United States was asking questions. Yet the news coming out of Panama, passed to relatives and friends, told a different story of the invasion than the one promoted by

---

1. While denied by the U.S. government and media for months, the widespread loss of life was finally acknowledged on September 30, 1990, on CBS-TV's "60 Minutes."

the Bush Administration—a story not of liberators being welcomed but of death and destruction. A story of a country of 2.5 million people, 90% Black, Mestizo and Indian, subjected once again to a U.S. military invasion.

In early January 1990, Ramsey Clark, former Attorney General of the United States, went to Panama City. He spoke with victims, witnesses, past and present officials, doctors, and clergy. He measured mass graves and saw the charred rubble that was all that was left of the working-class, mainly Black community of El Chorrillo.

While in Panama City, Mr. Clark challenged the Pentagon Southern Command's figure of civilian Panamanian deaths, which then, two weeks after the invasion, they were adamantly putting at 84. Within days, the Southern Command upped the number of Panamanians killed to 202 civilians and 314 military.

Mr. Clark characterized the aftermath of the invasion as a "conspiracy of silence." The media, which had been barred from the war areas for the first two days of the invasion, had simply echoed the news releases of the State Department, Pentagon and White House.

A picture was being painted at home of a kinder, gentler war, welcomed by all Panamanians. Those who defended their country, the Dignity Battalions made up of Panamanian volunteers, mostly from the poor neighborhoods and union committees, were branded as responsible for the almost total destruction of communities like El Chorrillo. When it was later shown that this was the result of U.S. bombing, rocket fire and house-to-house arson by soldiers, not a word was said in the U.S. media.

The whole thing, we were supposed to believe, had nothing in common with the 15 other blatantly imperialist invasions and military interventions of the United States into Panama between 1856 and 1989.

In mid-January, the Independent Commission of Inquiry on the U.S. Invasion of Panama was established by a politically diverse group of Panamanians, others from the Caribbean, and U.S. human rights activists, including attorneys, journalists and clergy. The Commission members firmly believe in the right to independence and sovereignty of every country, and have considerable collective knowledge and experience of U.S. involvement in the region.

The Commission set out first and foremost to listen to Panamanians themselves. It set up a flow of information from different cities and human rights organizations in Panama—leaders from different political back- grounds, community and union organizers, clergy, medical personnel, and the victims of the invasion themselves.

In addition to assisting Ramsey Clark in gathering information, the Commission sent investigators to Panama and interviewed many other observers who had travelled there. For months there were constant phone calls and an endless faxing of documents between the Commission office and Panama.

Despite arrests, firings and extreme difficulties, dozens of Panamanians risked all to bring to light the truth about the invasion. Hundreds of interviews were conducted by the National Human Rights Commission of Panama (CONADEHUPA). An umbrella organization of human rights groups throughout Central America (CODEHUCA) also sent its own investigating teams. With their permission, excerpts from their reports are included in this book.

Our Commission set as its fundamental task making public the truth about the deaths, destruction and suffering caused by the invasion—to break the conspiracy of silence. It sent preliminary reports on the situation to thousands of people all over the United States who were seeking information. Weekly, sometimes daily news releases went out to television, radio, and newspapers, small and large. The Commission undertook a relentless, activist, advocacy role when news of arrests was received, organizing pressure for the prisoners' release.

It made a U.S. government chart public that gives the names of State Department and Pentagon officials in charge of every ministry of the new Panamanian government.

All this, however, was not news as far as the media were concerned. Despite constant calls to the Commission office by journalists asking for information, the stories seldom got past the editor. We were often told, "Get us something hot and we'll run it." But the fact that the United States was running the new "democratic" Panamanian government wasn't the news they wanted. Thousands of Panamanian children left homeless was not fit for the 10 o'clock news. The Endara cabinet's links to the drug world were shrugged off.

A notable exception was the reporting of Pacifica (noncommercial radio) correspondent Robert Knight, who relentlessly pursued the truth on his program "Undercurrents."

Based on the information they were receiving, Panamanian investigators, leading citizens, clergy, human rights organizations, and the Commission estimated that thousands had died in the invasion. But none of these sources were interviewed or given a chance to tell their story to the mass media.

There was widespread obstruction of information by the Southern Command and the U.S.-installed Endara regime. Investigators were systematically denied access to files. Government officials and medical personnel were intimidated and repressed. The U.S. military has still not returned 15,000 boxes of Panamanian government documents stolen during the invasion, not even to its friends in the Presidential Palace.

But many people came forward on and off the record. Clergy heard privately from their congregations. Public workers compiled statistics. People spoke to those they trusted. And many more deaths than the official count were uncovered. Only those who discount the testimony of a farmer in Darien, a banana worker in Chiriquí, a domestic servant in San Miguel, an Indigenous person in Kuna Yala, a mother in El Chorrillo, a peddler in Colón, a doctor, a priest, a teacher, an ambulance driver, a relative of a military officer, or a high school student could go along with the U.S. military's version of what happened.

Perhaps the U.S. attitude is best typified by a press release issued January 12, 1990, by Les Aspin (D-CO), Chairman of the House Armed Services Committee. He praised the U.S. military forces and said, "We [the committee] heard no complaints from Panamanians about the indiscriminate use of firepower by U.S. troops."

To date neither the U.S. military, the Bush Administration, nor Congress has authorized compensation or a claims board for civilian victims of the invasion covering death, injury or destruction of property.

In May 1990, after 25 years of silence, the news broke that the Central Intelligence Agency (CIA) had assisted the Indonesian military in its horrifying massacres of nearly a million people in 1965-66.[2] At almost the same time, it was revealed to the world that the CIA had provided the information to the South African secret police that led to the arrest and 27-year imprisonment of Nelson Mandela.[3] A new book by Morley Safer[4] describes more U.S. atrocities in Vietnam.

Although now in the headlines, most of the information in these stories is not new. There were international tribunals, pamphlets, public forums and protests about all these events around the time they occurred. They were ignored by the major media and thus buried from public awareness for decades. The reports by the unofficial sources, both in those countries and in the United States, were disputed and impugned, just as they are doing now with regard to Panama.

President George Bush in his first public explanation of the invasion gave four reasons he said justified the action. He claimed then that it was 1) to protect U.S. lives; 2) to defend the Canal; 3) to restore democracy to

---

2. This excellent piece of investigative reporting by Kathy Kadane first appeared in the Spartanburg, SC, *Herald-Journal* on May 19 and then the *San Francisco Examiner* and *Washington Post* of May 20.

3. Cox News Service, June 10, 1990.

4. Morley Safer, *Flashbacks* (New York: Random House, 1990).

Panama; and 4) to stop drug trafficking and bring General Manuel Antonio Noriega to justice. But in fact the invasion destroyed many lives, U.S. and Panamanian; the Canal was never in danger; Panama today has a narrowly based, oligarchic government sworn in on a U.S. military base; and now the prosecution in Miami is admitting it has no hard evidence linking Noriega to drugs.[5]

But if these justifications are not true, what was the real motive for the U.S. invasion?

The Commission found all of Bush's justifications to be lies and deception, believed by no one in the U.S. government, and meant simply to gain support from the U.S. public, which disapproved of intervention in Central America.[6]

In 1977, General Omar Torrijos, the popular leader of Panama, signed three treaties with President Jimmy Carter. The treaties called for the Panama Canal to be turned over completely to Panama in the year 2000. In January of 1990, a Panamanian, appointed by Panama, would oversee the Canal Commission for the first time. *Most significantly, the treaties also called for the 14 U.S. bases in Panama to be returned to Panamanian control by the year 2000.*

Torrijos's grave site was desecrated and the Torrijos museum was ransacked during the invasion. Soon after the invasion, the name of the Torrijos Airport was changed. The Bush Administration then began saying its aim was to overthrow "21 years of dictatorship," going back to 1968 when General Torrijos came to power, in a military coup, as a result of the struggle for independence from the United States.

While the Panama Canal is extremely important to international commerce, it should be remembered that its functioning was never disrupted for 75 years until the U.S. invasion. To explain why the United States would go so far as to invade Panama to change the treaties, it is necessary to understand Panama's strategic military significance for the entire region.

Over the five years preceding the invasion, the United States had made many demands on Panama with which the Noriega regime increasingly refused to comply, notwithstanding Noriega's previous collaboration with U.S. agencies. The main demand was a renegotiation of the 1977 treaties in order to continue U.S. military bases past the year 2000.

The United States, through none other than Admiral John Poindexter

---

5. See p. 58, Report of the Commission of Inquiry.
6. See the Report of the Commission, pp. 19-61 of this book.

of Iran-Contra infamy, demanded repeatedly that Panama allow Nicaraguan counterrevolutionary forces to be based there. It further demanded that Panama end its economic and political cooperation with Nicaragua and Cuba. The significance of the timing of the invasion—just weeks before the Nicaraguan elections—should not be lost. It was a message: "This is what will happen to you too if you oppose us."

U.S. military operations are currently being conducted in Darien, the Panamanian province bordering Colombia and in Peru. Recent agreements between the Endara regime and the United States include putting the U.S. Coast Guard aboard every Panamanian vessel, prompting even the new Foreign Minister to call it an insult to Panama's sovereignty. It has been widely reported that secret discussions are underway to extend the leases of the U.S. bases, and in fact open new areas to the U.S. military. Since the invasion three military bases which had been returned to Panama have now been taken back by the U.S. Southern Command.

The invasion of Panama, U.S. military operations in Peru, Bolivia, Colombia—all are carried out on the pretext of the fight against drugs. This is one of the cruelest of deceptions. If this government really wants to fight the drug epidemic, why is it cutting funding for drug treatment centers here while spending $2 billion on the invasion? Why was public attention focused on Noriega as the culprit while the role of major U.S. banks in laundering huge amounts of drug money creates hardly a ripple?[7]

To achieve its goals, the United States for three years prior to the invasion tightened the economic noose around Panama's neck by imposing sanctions and seizing the government's assets. Promises of economic benefits to some were followed by threats to cut off pension payments to Canal workers. A hundred incidents by the U.S. military, including the temporary seizure of towns and setting up roadblocks, were intended to provoke a response by the Panamanian Defense Forces.

A massive media campaign to demonize General Noriega was launched, including obtaining his indictment in a U.S. court on drug charges. All of this was part of a deliberate and calculated plan to get General Noriega to either accede to U.S. demands or step aside. When military threats, economic sanctions and negotiations failed to produce the desired results, the United States invaded Panama.

Then came the unprecedented step of kidnapping a sovereign country's

---

7. For example, Bank of America was fined $4.5 million by the Treasury Department on Jan. 21, 1986, for failing to report more than 17,000 large cash transactions. The civil penalty was reported on the next day in a few papers like *The New York Times* and then quickly forgotten.

head of state to stand trial in a U.S. court that has no jurisdiction over him and not a shred of legal grounds for its actions.

The image of Panama under Noriega as a brutally totalitarian dictatorship does not stand up to scrutiny. While its policies sometimes favored the oligarchy, sometimes the poor, the Noriega regime allowed political opposition to exist on both left and right, as the testimonies in this book by Panamanians of various persuasions show. The effective affirmative action policy for Blacks, Mestizos and Indians started by Torrijos was continued under Noriega.

The U.S. establishment wasn't horrified when Noriega used force against demonstrators demanding the Shah of Iran get out of Panama, or when he attempted to cut back on union rights. But they were outraged when he repressed those U.S.-trained officers in the Panamanian Defense Forces (PDF) who attempted to overthrow his government, as well as the Panamanian political leaders who supported those attempts.

It is pure hypocrisy to say the invasion was to promote democracy in Panama and end a dictatorship. Washington's record in this area is one of support for the most murderous dictators, from Somoza in Nicaragua to Pinochet in Chile. U.S.-sponsored governments in El Salvador and Guatemala have killed hundreds of thousands of workers and peasants.

The Bush Administration wants us to believe that that was the old CIA, the old cold warriors. The U.S. government is different now. The world situation has changed so drastically, the argument goes, that the CIA, being no longer relevant, now dedicates itself to the establishment of democracy via humanitarian channels.

Yet Colonel Oliver North and Admiral John Poindexter, two war criminals guilty of selling weapons to arm the Contras and enrich themselves, are portrayed as misguided heroes. Then-President Ronald Reagan and now-President George Bush, former head of the CIA, are clearly implicated but go uncharged.

The new changes in the world situation, the so-called demise of East/West hostility, have led not to a lessening of U.S. military and CIA intervention, but to their increasing boldness. The U.S. Congress has once again given the green light to the CIA to assassinate heads of state.[8] There has been no let-up in U.S. funding and training of death squads in El

---

8. Former CIA general counsel Russell Bruemmer, speaking at an Albany, N.Y., law school symposium on April 5, 1990, said a Bush Administration policy review had determined that the "unintended" death of a foreign leader in operations like a hostage rescue or coup would not violate the presidential order in effect since 1975 that prohibits assassinations.

Salvador, Guatemala, Colombia, Mozambique and Angola.

There is a large build-up of U.S. forces throughout Latin America which is openly discussed by the Pentagon as necessary to contain "areas of unrest" caused by growing poverty throughout the region. The Coast Guard has fired upon a Cuban freighter flying a Panamanian flag, and has increased its economic squeeze and military threats against Cuba. Washington is demanding that Peru allow U.S. bases on its soil. And the budget for CIA activity has been increased, not cut.

Some would blame the people here for the government's reactionary policies. But Commission members believed that there was considerable opposition to the invasion in the U.S. Yet it was rendered invisible by the monolithic line of the media. So the Commission decided to organize an event that would let the Panamanian people speak to the people of North America about the invasion.

On April 5, 1990, over 2,000 people jammed New York City's Town Hall, overflowing onto 43rd Street where an auxiliary public address system was set up, to hear a variety of speakers from Panama tell the real story of the invasion for the first time in the United States.

The testimonies given in that program, "Voices from Panama," along with many others from additional sources, are presented in this book. We hope it will shed light on what really happened in Panama and why it happened, and most of all that it will encourage active opposition to U.S. military and economic aggression.

> Gavrielle Gemma
> Teresa Gutierrez
> *Project Directors*
> *Independent Commission of Inquiry*
> *June 20, 1990*

We Never Heard the Truth

*Former Attorney General Ramsey Clark's
speech to the April 5th Town Hall meeting.*

We're here to listen to Voices from Panama. Perhaps the single greatest problem we have on the planet is our inability to hear voices that know the truth and can set us free.

I'll speak softly. I want *their* voices to be heard and remembered. And I'll carry no stick. I'll speak first through voices of the past, a few voices *of* and other voices *about* Panama because so much of the whole struggle for human freedom is between memory and forgetting.

Let's go back nearly 500 years to an account in 1513 by a priest describing Balboa as he rushed into the Pacific Ocean—having shed his 15 kilograms of armor in all the lust of exploration and exploitation portending all the horrors they brought—and nearly drowned in the Gulf of San Miguel. A cross was carved on the beach. All those who were present were registered. And the other ocean was "discovered."

The following year in Darien, in 1514, a voice is recorded that speaks of the beauty of Panama. It wasn't clearly known yet, but it was sensed, that this was a bracelet of incredible beauty, full of jewels and riches, linking two continents. Gilberto Joviedo described the Panamanian fruits as being as glorious compared to the fruits of Europe as the feathers of a peacock are to the sparrows of the Spanish fields. He described the beauty of *los indios* with the same joy.

In 1541 comes one of the most important voices of history. It's a voice that reminds us powerfully that even from the beginning it was clearly seen how wrong the course of conquest was. It's the voice of Bartolomé de las Casas, recently appointed Bishop of Chiapas after 30 years of struggle for the rights of the Indian people of the New World. He issued his proclamation that every Indian is "free of right." He convinced Charles V of the Holy Roman Empire, who decreed it so. He persuaded two popes to do the same. He was, we are told, the most hated man in the Americas, hated by the colonials because he insisted that the Indian peoples here were equal to all peoples everywhere in dignity, in individuality, and in right. And he refused absolution in his church to anyone who owned Indians.

Already the exploitation of Indians was the dominant human and economic fact of the New World. Consider only the Valley of Mexico, which probably was home, in one of the most naturally beautiful places on earth, to 2 million people. Within three generations of the arrival of Cortés, the Indian population was down to 70,000.

Meanwhile, across the Atlantic in the port of Luanda in the present country of Angola, the Portuguese were loading onto their ships the Blacks they had captured in nets. They had been marched through the jungles and over the plains, past the heartbreaking drums of their villages. They had ropes around their necks linking them to each other, and were branded. Before they boarded canoes to be carried to ships that would take them across the Atlantic, salt was placed on their tongues and water sprinkled on their heads and they were given a Christian name. They were told that they were now the children of God.

Many died on the voyage or later of what was once called melancholia, heartbreak from yearning for what you knew and loved. And they were told to forget forever the name and the spirit of Shango and all that meant so much to them from their earliest memories.

The next voice of Panama is about an Englishman, Henry Morgan. More than 300 years ago Henry Morgan, after having overwhelmed the fortress of Portobelo, entered the City of Panama with 2,000 soldiers. The night turned into day, we are told, from the fires in the city. Homes, hospitals, convents and churches were torched by the men who marched behind the flag of England. Morgan proclaimed, "We came here for money, not for prayer." It was 1671 and the City of Panama was destroyed.

Leaping forward to 1857, the railroad link from the Atlantic to the Pacific was completed and we hear of a former captain of the Texas Rangers with the improbable initials and almost improbable name, Ron Ruggles. He had been hired as chief of security for the railroad. He shot a Panamanian in the heart. Not even a Texas Ranger could handle the hurt of the Panamanian people, and on September 19, 1851, there came the first significant U.S. military intervention in Panama. Two warships landed 160 United States Marines.

Between 1850 and 1860 there were four major invasions, primarily by veterans of the Mexican-American War on the Spanish-dominated island of Cuba. The President of the Confederacy, Jefferson Davis, was importuned to lead one. Surely after the Civil War, he wished he had, but fate destined him for other things.

At the same time that our Marines first went into Panama, William Walker was marching from Granada toward what was to become Managua to proclaim himself King of Nicaragua. His first two official acts were to reinstate slavery abolished since the Confederation of Central America, which had lasted until 1838, and to make English, which few other than Walker spoke, the official language.

In 1856, at the Democratic National Convention in Baltimore, a United States Senator from New York urged a plank in the platform that supported extending the Kingdom of Nicaragua, under the leadership of William Walker, from Mexico to Colombia.

We were looking for territory to expand slavery. We concealed our intentions even then. The Ostend Manifesto of 1857, which remained secret until 1927, was a direct threat against Spain if it did not sell us Cuba. Even the Ostend Manifesto was two generations after Thomas Jefferson suggested we "pluck the Cuban apple from the Spanish tree."

Graham Greene described Panama as "the conception of a single person." He understood perfectly well that there were several million people who knew otherwise. He was speaking only of that particular moment when Teddy Roosevelt realized he didn't need to fight all of Colombia if he could spin off Panama and take it over. And that's just what he did.

There was one difference between the leadership of Roosevelt and the leadership we have now. He said what he thought most of the time. Asked once by what right he acquired the territory on which he placed the canal, he said, "I took it."

We should never forget the powerful poem "To Roosevelt" by Rubén Darío written in 1903. New York is prominently mentioned in it. Even the Lady in the Harbor, called almost that, is mentioned when he describes her light shining on our easy conquests. He speaks of Roosevelt and America as the *fuerte cazador,* the powerful hunter, the *riflero terrible,* the terrorist rifleman. He described the "conspiracy of Hercules": power, and the "conspiracy of Mammon": greed, as the spirit of America. He concludes, speaking of the people from the United States, but with Roosevelt as the symbol, that he, and therefore we, lacked only one thing: "Dios," by which he meant soul. Where is your soul? Where is your compassion?

During this century there was a major U.S. intervention in Panama every time independence was seriously asserted. And for all of those years, across that beautiful bracelet that links the continents, there was this terrible scar, like a chain across the human heart, the intrusion on sovereignty and fundamental political, economic and human rights: the canal. It has dominated the lives of the people of Panama for all of this century.

And finally we come to December 20, 1989. We waited. We shouldn't have. We watched when action was called for. We were silent though many enjoyed the demonization period that we've witnessed so many times in so many places. We heard all of the false reasons being developed for what was going to happen, something anyone could sense.

We heard nothing said about the purpose of the invasion being instruction in absolute obedience to authority. We heard nothing about how "There will be no sovereignty in this hemisphere but ours." We heard nothing about the Southern Command being very comfortable in its quarters in Panama. We heard nothing about keeping the Canal, and our investment there. We heard nothing about the real reasons. We saw domestic politics, face saving and all those pitiful things impel us toward the invasion of Panama and its celebration.

We heard a bunch of lies. We never heard the truth.

There is no need to cite article and verse of the laws prohibiting the invasion. It would only distract from the obvious. Of course the invasion of Panama violated international law. One nation cannot invade another because of its displeasure with policies, or leadership there. Of course it violated the laws of the United States. We cannot under our law deploy military force in time of peace; killing civilians at the whim of the executive. And as you can imagine it violated the laws of the sovereign Republic of Panama which intend to protect its independence. But it also violated the human rights of millions of people, not just Panamanians but everyone affected and implicated, then, now and hereafter.

It was a physical assault of stunning violence. It was a time for testing new equipment with no concern for human lives. It was a time for measuring the worth of technology against the life of a child. The Stealth fighter in Panama! And now we hear, well, they didn't mean to hurt anybody.

How many times will we accept that sort of misinformation? You go to Panama right after the invasion, you go to a place like El Chorrillo, a "little stream" or "rush of water." At one time it was El Chorro, a lot of water. The people there before Cristobal Colón and the Mayflower enjoyed that water, it was *pura,* it was *sabrosa,* it was healthy. After the cut for the canal it came down to a trickle, and it's where the poor people were left to live.

I stayed in El Chorrillo in 1946 for a few weeks, just shortly after I got out of—yes!—the United States Marine Corps as a corporal. Like some of the older people from Panama, I spent some good nights in Kelly's Ritz and a few other places and I loved El Chorrillo and I loved its people— their diversity, their beauty, their joy, their music and their poetry. I couldn't believe it when I went back two weeks after our invasion and saw it in utter ruin: 15 blocks or more, home to at least 30,000 people, destroyed or so badly damaged that no one could possibly live there.

Try to imagine being there in the middle of the night, in the poor part of town, perhaps in a highrise, and all of a sudden the power is off. And then you hear artillery. And then you hear helicopters. And then you hear rockets. And then you hear heavy caliber automatic gunfire.

What do you do? You get under the bed, you hide where you can. How do you get out? Where do you go? What's going on? Where is it safe?

How many died? Doesn't anybody care how many people we killed in Panama?

General Stiner—who seemed to be the source of most public utterances on the subject of the invasion, how fine it was, how surgical and all the rest—was telling the press 84 Panamanian civilians killed as late as January 4th. Voltaire, you remember, argued the terrible thought that "history is fiction agreed upon." Napoleon loved that. He thought Voltaire was a pretty smart fellow.

The U.S. military wanted to make 84 Panamanian civilian deaths a fiction that history would agree on. But it's not going to work.

I estimated when I left in early January at least a thousand killed. There were probably several thousand. The people of the United States have an absolute moral obligation to demand the most thorough account possible.

Let me wind up with two things.

I kept hearing about a place called Jardín de Paz. Sounded nice—the garden of peace. And I went out there the last evening I was in Panama, which was the first Saturday of January of this year, and found a couple of little children who played in the cemetery because it was the best place they had to play. I gave one of them a dollar (Americans should know that the currency in Panama is the dollar; they don't have a currency of their own) and asked if he had seen anybody burying any bodies around there. And he took me and several Panamanian companions over to what seemed to be the gravesite. I paced it off. The grave was 18 feet wide—six paces. It was 120 feet long—40 paces. The earth hadn't been filled in for an additional 26 paces. The unfilled cut was five feet deep.

We need to know how many Panamanians were killed in the invasion. The families are entitled to know what's happened to their loved ones, to their children, to their women, to their men. And most of all, and I say this to the people from the United States, we live in a country that functions to some minor degree under democratic institutions, and whether it does or not, we are responsible for the acts of our agents. We need to pull up our socks, we need to find out everything that happened here. Then we must resolve that it shall never happen again!

Not in Panama, not in Nicaragua, not in Cuba, not in Haiti, not in Syria or Iraq. Nowhere!

We have some folks at home that need help. Let's lend a hand here. They are victims of the same false values. But we must recognize that we have a responsibility to see that the anthem of Panama is fulfilled and that victory belongs to the people of Panama at last.

Philip Agee

Only the Latest and Not the Last

In 1975, former CIA officer Philip Agee dismayed the agency by publishing an insider's account of how it functioned to subvert and undermine progressive and nationalist forces and governments in Latin America. His book Inside the Company, *which named CIA agents and their front organizations in many countries, quickly became a best-seller.*

More than 25 years ago, on July 11, 1963, Ecuadorean military officers overthrew President Carlos Julio Arosemena and his government. Elected Vice President in 1960, Arosemena had succeeded to the presidency in 1961 when José María Velasco resigned under military pressure. Upon deposing Arosemena, the military put him on an aircraft and sent him into exile in Panama.

The 1963 coup, which we in the CIA helped provoke, was followed immediately by repression of leftist and nationalist political movements and eventually by five years of military rule. Reading my account of those events, which I detailed ten years later in *Inside the Company,*[1] reminds me once again how little the methods of repression have changed. We see them applied daily in the U.S. "pacification" of Panama.

We wanted Arosemena out because he refused to crack down on our enemies, and he resisted joining our crusade against the Cuban revolution and its considerable influence in Latin America. In this, the military junta that replaced Arosemena was only too eager to comply.

---

1. Philip Agee, *Inside the Company: CIA Diary* (New York, Stonehill Publishing Co., 1975).

15

One of our first actions after Arosemena's overthrow was to pass previously prepared "enemies lists" to our police and military collaborators for arrests and interrogations. I was in charge of the lists, a requirement for every CIA Station in the region and known in characteristic language as the "Subversive Control Watch List." On each subject the list contained up-to-date photographs, biographical data and information on places of residence, work, leisure activities, children's schools, relatives and anything else that would assist in swift arrest at a given moment. Within days the jails were overflowing. When I read of CIA-prepared lists being used by the U.S. military for arrests in Panama, I thought: Well sure, still at it.

Then, when I learned of interrogations of Panamanians by U.S. Special Forces, I recalled how we brought in an interrogation team of Special Forces, Spanish-speaking people from the United States who could pass as Latin Americans, to work with our police and military counterparts in interrogations of those arrested from our lists. The team came from its permanent base in Panama, and I reviewed each interrogation report for information of value and follow-up questioning. The "take," of course, served for planning recruitments of possible spies from among the prisoners, and it found its way, properly indexed for retrieval, into our files for future use.

In preparation for the coup, we had followed the normal procedure in demonizing, as occurred with General Noriega, the person we wanted removed. This we did through paid agents in the local media and through the political forces that we financed. We also falsified documents that compromised our enemies and made certain they were published. Not least, we helped organize and finance opposition civic fronts, such as one called the National Defense Front, for mobilizing large crowds in street actions. In these fronts we counted on organizations of women, students, trade unions, sectors of the Catholic Church and many others, all of whom, naturally, we influenced through our media campaign.

All that was still standard practice, I thought, on reading of the CIA's $10 million intervention in the 1989 Panamanian elections and the street demonstrations of the so-called Civic Crusade. I could also imagine the congratulations among CIA officers when the lynching atmosphere created by the Civic Crusade at the Papal Nuncio's residence provoked General Noriega's surrender.

Of course, the U.S. invasion and occupation of Panama has gone much further than our intervention long ago in Ecuador. We did succeed in temporarily weakening our enemies, but we had simply no way, nor need really, to impose total control as has occurred in Panama. We had no need to turn the clock back 20 years, as in Panama, no need to reimpose minority racist rule, no need to overturn treaties on waterways or U.S. military bases.

When the 1963 Ecuadorean coup occurred, the public impact in the United States was less than a leaf falling from a tree. How different from Panama! In this case the U.S. public had to be subjected to several years' preparation through, as usual, demonization of the enemy. In the event CIA intervention in the electoral process failed (as it did), and invasion was necessary (as it was), people in the United States would need pre-conditioning in order to accept the loss of U.S. lives. With a little help from the U.S. media, it worked.

In the aftermath, the U.S. media has been just as helpful in covering up in the United States the human cost to Panamanians: in deaths and injuries, in homes destroyed, in arrests and concentration camps, in numbers and conditions of refugees, in workers' dismissals and repression of trade unions, in political vendettas, and in the brutality of the U.S. military and their continuing "pacification" operations. No ministry of propaganda could be more effective than the official U.S. media are, as they consign the occupation of Panama to non-news, in preventing mass outrage in the United States.

The end of the Cold War may be proclaimed on every street corner, but Panama shows that the North-South dimension of the conflict rages on—and not between the United States and "communists," but between this country and those to the South who refuse to follow U.S. dictates. In an age when transparency and restructuring have brought profound and in some ways positive change in countries once considered the enemy, we wait in vain for any such "new thinking" to emerge in official Washington.

Instead, we see U.S. military forces reorganizing for more "Third World" interventions, as in Panama, and the underlying definition of "U.S. interests" remains the same: control of foreign resources, markets and labor. "Narco-terrorism" may replace "International Communism" as the enemy, but getting rid of the Arosemenas and Noriegas, and anyone else who resists, is still the order of the day.

This book, compiled by the Independent Commission of Inquiry, will help break the information blockade on Panama, and should stimulate people in the United States to join those already working to bring out the truth and to assist the victims of this most recent, but by no means last, U.S. disgrace. Looming just over the horizon are military actions against Cuba, of which the human and material costs are incalculable.

Solidarity not only means mobilizing public pressure to end the occupation and total U.S. intervention in Panama. It also means ending the travel ban and economic blockade against Cuba, as well as stopping the constant U.S. provocations: naval and air maneuvers off Cuban coasts and at Guantanamo, Radio and TV Martí, and attacks against Cuban shipping.

This book will also help all of us to understand that the real enemies of the people of the United States are not in Panama, or in Cuba, or in any other "Third World" country. They are right here, at home, and they are led by George Bush, a man whose own "unclean hands" should render any U.S. case against Manuel Antonio Noriega both a legal and political farce the world over. "Bush-Noriega: Get the Connection!"

Report of the Independent Commission of Inquiry

Events Leading up to the Invasion

After two years of economic strangulation failed to topple the Panamanian government, the U.S. government resorted to a massive military invasion to accomplish its objectives. What were the reasons for the preoccupation with Panama? Reading the daily newspapers in the United States in the months before the invasion, one got the unmistakable impression that the Pentagon was building up to the inevitable use of military force. But what for?

The headlines demonizing General Noriega were designed to psychologically prepare the population for the need to send U.S. GIs to kill and be killed. But careful observers of U.S. foreign policy know that U.S. support for dictatorial and corrupt governments in other countries in Central America indicates that there must be some other motivation to explain the decision by the Bush Administration to go to war.

Ample evidence reveals that the U.S. government and the Pentagon planned to overthrow the Panamanian government and replace it with a dependent and subservient regime(s) which would renegotiate the key provisions of the 1977 Panama Canal Treaties.[1] These provisions—the shutdown in 1999 of all 14 U.S. Southern Command bases in Panama—are the section of the Treaties most objectionable to U.S. military planners and also most vital to the decades-long struggle of the Panamanian people to achieve genuine sovereignty.

It is important to remember that Ronald Reagan campaigned actively

---

1. For example, see the letter of March 26, 1987, from J. Edward Fox, Assistant Secretary of State for Legislative and Intergovernmental Affairs, to Senator Jesse Helms (R-NC) reproduced on the following page.

MAR 2 6 1987

Dear Senator Helms:

The State Department shares your view that when the Carter-Torrijos treaties are being renegotiated, the prolongation of the U.S. military presence in the Panama Canal area till well after the year 2000 should be brought up for discussion. The continuing power of the Sandinistas in Nicaragua, the activities of the Salvadoran insurgents and the influence of communist Cuba in the region make it urgently necessary for the United States to strengthen its position in Central America.

The continuing polarization of the political forces in Panama may lead to a crisis in the country which would pose a serious threat to stability in the region. The State Department is of the opinion that in order to avoid such a situation, steps should be taken to bring about the resignation of General Noriega as Commander-in-Chief of the National Guard and to set up an interim government, consisting of sober-minded politicians and senior military officers, which sees as its principal aims the promotion of the process of democratization and the safeguarding of U.S. strategic interests.

I want you to know that the importance of these problems is fully appreciated in the White House and here, in the State Department, and that effective steps will be taken to solve them.

Sincerely,

J. Edward Fox
Assistant Secretary
Legislative and Intergovernmental Affairs

The Honorable
Jesse A. Helms,
United States Senate.

Letter from the State Department to Senator Jesse Helms.

against the Panama Canal Treaties as early as 1977, when he was positioning himself for his 1980 presidential bid.[2] Particularly onerous to Reagan was the shutdown of U.S. bases. Was Reagan speaking only for himself or for a larger section of right-wing opinion, particularly the Committee on the Present Danger and other right-wing think tanks that are strongly rooted in the Pentagon and the military-industrial complex?

Protecting the economic interests of U.S. corporations and banks in Panama, which are linked to shipping and commerce because of the Canal as well as to Panama's banking sector, were also big concerns for the United States during the Reagan-Bush years. But we believe that the primary goal of the destabilization and later invasion of Panama was to ensure that the Southern Command would have long-term access to forward bases that could project U.S. military power in Colombia, Peru, El Salvador, Guatemala, and throughout Latin America and the Caribbean.[3]

Although Reagan and significant sectors of the Pentagon establishment always considered the signing of the 1977 Canal Treaties (signed by President Jimmy Carter and General Omar Torrijos) to be a "mistake,"[4] Panama did not occupy center stage in the Reagan-Bush Central America agenda in the early 1980s. Instead, the United States was pouring in hundreds of millions of dollars to create the Contra army from remnants of Somoza's National Guard in Nicaragua. The Reagan-Haig-Casey foreign policy team carried out a campaign of similar magnitude to prop up the right-wing death-squad regime in El Salvador.

This is not to say that the Reagan Administration was not interested in Panama. During the early 1980s, U.S. intelligence capabilities in Panama were significantly upgraded to the point where all of Central America and most of South America could be monitored from U.S. facilities there.[5] Since it could function as a base for reconnaissance planes, a listening post for the National Security Agency (NSA), and headquarters for the Southern Command, Panama provided an "intelligence feast" for U.S. military planners.[6]

Many charged that the United States may have involved itself covertly

---

2. See *The New York Times,* August 26, 1977, p. 1, and Reagan fund-raising letter on p. 128 of this book.

3. Brig. Gen. Robin G. Tornow, U.S. Air Force commander in Panama at the time of the invasion, said, "Our main purpose here is to organize, train and equip forces to support the defense of the Panama Canal, protect U.S. lives and maintain a forward base." Tornow was quoted in the pro-Endara paper *Panamá Libre* of the third week of May, 1990.

4. See Reagan fund-raising letter, page 128.

5. *Covert Action Information Bulletin (CAIB),* #34, Summer 1990.

6. Seymour Hersh, *The New York Times,* June 12, 1986.

in domestic Panamanian politics as well. In 1981, General Omar Torrijos died in a plane crash under suspicious circumstances. There have been many charges that the CIA and the Southern Command were involved in the destruction of the Torrijos plane. In 1987, the CIA, which routinely refuses comment about its involvement in covert operations, took the unusual step of denying that the agency "had been involved in the incident."[7] The CIA announcement followed a day of student rioting that was precipitated by an allegation by a high-ranking member of the Panamanian Defense Forces (PDF) that the United States had conspired to plant a bomb on the Torrijos aircraft.

Between mid-1985 and 1986 there began a noticeable change in the Reagan Administration's attitude toward the Panamanian government.

The U.S. government's shift to outright hostility was signaled by a U.S. media campaign starting in late 1985 directed against General Noriega. According to Noriega's version, the souring of U.S.-Panamanian relations started after he refused U.S. demands to use Panama as a staging ground for military attacks against Nicaragua. Although it is not possible to confirm Noriega's assertion from independent sources, the Reagan Administration's "obsession" with overthrowing the Sandinista government in Nicaragua is well known. When the Administration was barred from aiding the Contras by Congressional restraints, it pursued a worldwide campaign to line up and win the financial and logistical assistance of "friendly" countries. Is it hard to imagine Reagan, John Poindexter, Oliver North, *et al.* resorting to bullying tactics against a small nation in Central America that defied the United States on the question of Nicaragua?

Although all the facts behind the falling out between the United States and Noriega may not be revealed for decades, if ever, it is obvious that the Panamanian government was early on treated to a bad press campaign in major media outlets, starting with the October 8, 1985, *The New York Times* editorial that warned, "General Noriega should not underestimate U.S. strategic interests in Panama's future."

In addition to conflict about Nicaragua, the Panamanian government took other positions that were interpreted as hostile to U.S. foreign policy aims in the region and, moreover, indicative of a growing nationalist and independent stance by Noriega and the Panamanian Defense Forces (PDF) officer corps. Specifically, Panama stopped the Salvadoran government from utilizing Panamanian facilities like Gorgas Hospital, which had been used to treat Salvadoran government soldiers wounded in combat with the leftist guerrillas of the Faribundo Martí Front for National Liberation (FMLN). This decision followed mass street protests against the Salvadoran government.

---

7. *CAIB,* op. cit.

Panama also refused to end trade with Cuba and to deny Cuba access to the Canal. Panama was an area where Cuba could purchase goods otherwise hard to obtain because of the 30-year-long U.S. economic blockade. The Reagan Administration must have been alarmed that Panama, a country it considered "belonged" to the United States,[8] made an agreement in 1977 with the Soviet Union to give landing rights to Aeroflot and to set up a commercial entity providing dry docks for Soviet fishing vessels in both the Atlantic and Pacific oceans.

Economic and Political Warfare

During the three years prior to the invasion, the United States conducted massive sabotage of the Panamanian economy. The goal of this campaign was to force a change in policy by the Panamanian government or a relinquishing of power by Noriega. In March 1988, Draconian economic sanctions were imposed. These included freezing $56 million of Panamanian assets in U.S. banks; excluding Panama from the U.S. sugar import quota; refusing to pay taxes and fees owed to Panama by the United States for the Canal; and prohibiting commercial trade with Panama.

The imposition of economic sanctions created a run on Panamanian banks. To stem the crisis, they closed for two months and 500,000 savings accounts with a value of about $270 million were frozen, creating severe hardships for many Panamanians. These savings accounts were unfrozen four months after the invasion.[9]

In 1989, the United States moved to exclude from U.S. ports any ship bearing Panamanian registry, a move that deprived Panama of a major source of income and disrupted international commerce. Arranging for even routine international credit became difficult since an embargoed Panama found itself unable to pay debt service on loans from the International Monetary Fund (IMF), the World Bank and others.

The U.S. Treasury Department maintained a list of hundreds of Panamanians with whom transacting business was prohibited. The Treasury Department, citing the Trading with the Enemy Act, put on the list those Panamanians who allegedly conducted trade with Cuba. Additionally, the State Department maintained a list of hundreds of Panamanians excluded from coming to the United States by an executive order of the President.

The combination of sanctions, embargoes and internal economic

---

8. During the 1976 Presidential campaign, Ronald Reagan boasted of the Canal to his jingoist supporters: "We bought it, we paid for it, it's ours, and we are going to keep it." From Ronnie Dugger, *On Reagan: The Man and His Presidency* (New York: McGraw-Hill Book Co., 1983), p. 362.

9. United Press International dispatch of April 17, 1990.

sabotage caused a $500 million loss to the Panamanian economy and a whopping 27% contraction in the country's Gross National Product. This economic destabilization resulted in widespread unemployment—rising to about 30% of the entire workforce—prior to the invasion. The economic contraction was felt by all classes, but had a particularly devastating effect on the poorest Panamanians.

While creating social discontent through economic strangulation, the Pentagon raised its psychological pressure by steadily increasing military provocations.

The 1977 Canal Treaties prohibited the use of U.S. military forces outside the Canal Zone and U.S. military bases. Yet over 100 instances of U.S. military provocations in 1989 were documented by the Panamanian government. These included U.S. troops setting up roadblocks, searching Panamanian citizens, confronting PDF forces, occupying small towns for a number of hours, buzzing Panamanian air space with military aircraft, and surrounding public buildings with troops.

The United States also violated the 1977 Treaties by gradually deploying thousands of additional troops into Panama. The Treaties expressly froze the number of U.S. troops in Panama at the number in place at the time they were signed.

The United States set up private communications and support for forces aiming to topple the government of Panama. On October 3, 1989, an attempted coup, which received logistical backing from Southern Command forces, was thwarted by loyal PDF forces.

One week prior to the killing of a U.S. lieutenant colonel outside the headquarters of the PDF, a PDF soldier was wounded by U.S. troops. The killing of the U.S. officer was used as a pretext for the long-planned invasion. The front-page story of *The New York Times* on December 19, 1989 (the morning before the invasion) is headlined "President Calls Panama Slaying a Great Outrage." The Bush Administration insisted that the invasion was a response to this slaying and other alleged Panamanian provocations. Saving endangered American lives and property became the battle cry, as it was in Grenada and in the scores of U.S. interventions in Latin America during the past century. In fact, the preparations for the invasion were made well in advance. *Newsweek* validated the Panamanian claim that the slain U.S. officer was probably on an intelligence mission in preparation for the coming attack: "In the weeks before the invasion, officers posing as tourists visited the parts of Panama they would attack."[10]

The CIA ran numerous overt and covert operations in Panama prior to the invasion. These included a CIA-operated radio station run by an

---

10. *Newsweek,* June 25, 1990.

American, Kurt Muse, inside Panama. Muse was arrested by the Panamanian government, but was freed the night of the invasion by an elite unit of the 82nd Airborne Division that attacked the prison, killing and wounding many Panamanian prison guards.[11]

The U.S. government also organized and financed the opposition Civic Crusade, and hand picked its leaders: Guillermo Endara, Guillermo "Billy" Ford, and Ricardo Arias Calderón. These three became the new president and vice presidents, taking the oath of office at a U.S. military base the night of the invasion.

During the presidential election in May 1989, the CIA spent at least $10 million in U.S. taxpayers' money (a conservative figure) to finance the campaign of Guillermo Endara. This is an enormous sum when one considers that Panama's population is only 2.5 million. It is the per capita equivalent of a foreign government spending over $1,000,000,000 to influence a U.S. national election (five times the amount spent by George Bush and Michael Dukakis combined in the 1988 presidential election). Of course, it is illegal for U.S. candidates to receive foreign funding.

Furthermore, voters realized that a victory for the pro-Noriega candidate meant a guarantee that U.S. economic sanctions would remain in place, with all their attendant misery. Not exactly an atmosphere for a free election.

Although it did not support General Noriega, the Organization of American States (OAS) refused to validate the May 1989 elections. This is important because the United States contended that the December 20 invasion was aimed at "restoring democracy" and justified its installation of Guillermo Endara as president on the basis that he had been the rightful victor in the May 1989 elections.

Complaining that the United States had tried to "buy" and manipulate the elections, the Panamanian National Assembly on September 30, 1989, appointed a provisional president and vice-president and declared General Noriega head of state. The National Assembly was engaged in setting up new elections, assisted by the OAS. The opposition refused to take part.

It is also interesting to note that during the first five months of 1989, almost up to the eve of the May elections, the Bush Administration was engaged in a complex series of negotiations with the Noriega government. Some of these negotiations even took place inside State Department offices in Washington, D.C. According to sources who participated in the negotiations, the Bush Administration prepared a draft Federal Court order dismissing the February 1988 drug indictment against General Noriega in return for key concessions from the Panamanian government. According

---

11. Ibid.

to these same sources, the negotiations broke down prior to the May 1989 election when the Panamanian side refused to permit U.S. military base rights to be extended past the year 2000.

In their initial justification for the invasion, the Bush Administration made much about a purported "declaration of war" by General Noriega. In fact, neither General Noriega nor the Panamanian National Assembly ever declared war against the United States. This should not be too surprising since Panama's Defense Forces, numbering only 16,000 including local police, had at their disposal only two combat-ready divisions with about 3,000 soldiers. What the Panamanian Assembly passed on December 15, 1989, was a resolution that the country was "in a state of war." The resolution said nothing about an intent on the part of Panama to attack the United States or its citizens. Rather, the Assembly noted that U.S. military participation in the unsuccessful October 1989 coup attempt had created conditions equaling a "state of war." The intent of this measure is clear: not to menace the United States, but to alert the Panamanian people to the imminent danger of an invasion.

Death and Destruction Caused by the Invasion

In all armed conflicts, the rights of the parties in conflict to select the means and methods of war are not without limits. Two fundamental norms are derived from this principle. First, it is prohibited to use weapons, projectiles, materials, or methods of war not justified by military necessity. Secondly, parties in conflict are required to guarantee the respect and protection of civilian population and property and to make a distinction at all times between civil and combatant population as well as between civilian property and military targets. ... Attacks on civilians and civilian property are prohibited in all acts of violence, offensive or defensive. ... The prohibition includes indiscriminate attacks.

Geneva Conventions Additional Protocol, 1983

The U.S. military strategy in Panama totally violated the Geneva Conventions in order to overcome the single biggest threat to the invasion plans. There was both a reason and a method to the madness.

The Bush Administration felt compelled to employ "disproportionate use of force" and indiscriminate attacks on civilian populations. Why? Because there were overriding political reasons that required that the war be ended quickly and with few U.S. casualties.

Although there was never a question that the U.S. military would prevail in a war with Panama, the U.S. Administration did face a number of potentially serious problems. First, the invasion was so patently illegal that it was roundly condemned by the United Nations, the Organization of American States,[12] and most nations in the world. Thus, the United States risked worldwide isolation just at a time when the crisis in Eastern Europe opened up new geopolitical opportunities for U.S. foreign policy.

The other two potential problems faced by the Administration were far more serious. The sight of another "Yankee invasion" into Latin America had the predictable effect of creating a firestorm of condemnation and protest amongst the masses of Latin America. A protracted war, where occupying U.S. troops engaged nationalist guerrillas and their supporters among the civilian poor, would undoubtedly arouse mass movements of protest throughout the countries of the continent. Given the precarious character of many of the governments in Latin America, saddled with billions in debt to U.S. banks and reluctantly carrying out IMF-imposed austerity measures, the potential for sweeping political destabilization is obvious. This was of no small concern to the Bush Administration, which would suffer the political consequences if U.S. banks were unable to receive payment on their loans to Mexico, Argentina, Brazil, Venezuela and the others. Massive loans to Latin America had been the key to U.S. banking strategy in the 1970s. When one considers that 286 commercial banks in the United States have failed since 1989, the status of the $500 billion in bank loans to all of Latin America has to assume monumental importance for the well-being of the entire financial system.

Finally, the Bush Administration was undoubtedly fearful of a return of what Ronald Reagan called the "Vietnam Syndrome." This strange affliction gripped the people in the United States, who, after initially supporting the U.S. war effort in Vietnam, became its implacable foes as the war dragged on and more and more young GIs came home in body bags. The Bush Administration's quarantining of U.S. reporters so that they would be unable to witness and record the worst of the carnage in Panama indicated just how much it wanted the people in the United States kept ignorant of the brutal nature of the war. But even more important than the outright management of the news, the Administration was acutely aware that a protracted conflict and large numbers of U.S. casualties would inevitably lead to a polarization in U.S. society.

Thus, the military strategy for the invasion was designed to minimize U.S. casualties by employing overwhelming and superior forces simultaneously against all perceived pro-government strongholds. Disproportionate use of force and "overkill" were the hallmark of a strategy aimed at quickly crushing the armed opposition and intimidating pro-government supporters.

Unfortunately for the unsuspecting civilians living in Panama's poorest communities, where nationalist sentiment was high, this meant taking the

---

12. See OAS resolution, page 124.

brunt of an all-out military attack. On the night of December 19, while they were finishing the day's chores or relaxing after another long day, and after the children were already in bed, the residents of El Chorrillo were suddenly on the front lines of the largest U.S. military action since the Vietnam War. Their testimonies, which have been collected by the Independent Commission of Inquiry and by human rights organizations in Panama, tell a chilling and heart-rending story.[13]

The invasion was carried out by 24,000 U.S. troops armed with the most sophisticated weaponry and aircraft, including the Stealth fighter bomber. Many independent analysts felt that the Pentagon took the invasion as an opportunity to experiment with some of its newest high-tech weapons in a real battlefield situation. But no, we learn from Secretary of Defense Richard Cheney that the Stealth fighter bomber was used to *save* lives. "The reason we used that particular aircraft is because of its great accuracy. We dropped, I believe, two 2,000-pound bombs near Río Hato to pave the way for the Rangers when they landed there and to stun and disorient the [Panamanian troops]. And it worked because it reduced both Panamanian and U.S. casualties."[14] Really?

The invasion force used mortars, bazookas, artillery, tanks, M-60 machine guns, AC-130H Spectre gunships equipped with 105-mm howitzers, twin 20-mm Vulcan cannons (capable of 2,500 rounds a minute), 40-mm Bofors cannons (capable of 100 rounds a minute), the supersonic plane SR-71, Apache helicopters, and the Stealth fighter bomber.

Nine of the ten doctors on duty at Santo Tomás hospital at the time of the invasion were soon fired, arrested, or in hiding after having been labeled "Noriega supporters." The United States knew that their first-hand testimonies would be powerful rebuttal to U.S. propaganda about the "clean" and almost "casualty-free" nature of the invasion.

In the first 13 hours of the invasion, the United States dropped 422 bombs on Panama City.[15] In the poor neighborhood of El Chorrillo, which was leveled during the assault, almost all of the buildings were wooden structures.

Against the U.S. force, the Panamanian Defense Forces numbered about 15,000-16,000. But a great number of these were only trained and equipped to carry out police functions. The PDF contained only two combat-ready divisions, the Year 2000 Battalion and the Peace Battalion, with a combined troop strength of about 3,000. The Dignity Battalions,

---

13. See the "Voices from Panama" and "Additional Testimonies" sections of this book.

14. *Tropic Times,* December 27, 1989, newspaper of the U.S. Southern Command.

15. "Special Report on Activity on December 20, 1989" by Professor Nydia Cardoze, Director of the Institute of Geosciences, and Lic. Jaime Toral Bontet, UPA Seismological Station, Institute of Geosciences, University of Panama.

the pro-Noriega civilian militia, numbered about 3,000, of whom only a part were armed with rifles. Panama had a very small air force, no tanks, and only a patrol-boat navy.

U.S. military forces systematically destroyed all PDF buildings throughout the country, including the women's military training school. This was carried out by artillery fire and air attacks.

The Panamanian Constitution states that every citizen has a duty to defend the country from a foreign invasion. The PDF soldiers and the civilian militias who fought back were carrying out their obligations as Panamanians. This is important because the U.S. press frequently cites the figure "some 200" Panamanians killed, as though the young Panamanian soldiers who died fighting against incredible odds were not also murdered by foreign invaders.

The Terror of December 20-22

The assault on Panama, particularly on its poor neighborhoods, was of stunning violence. The National Human Rights Commission of Panama (CONADEHUPA), the Commission for the Defense of Human Rights in Central America (CODEHUCA), and the Independent Commission of Inquiry have collected hundreds of testimonies from the victims of the invasion.

The following account is from a young mother living in an El Chorrillo apartment with her seven-year-old son:

> I was ironing when I heard the first sound of machine guns firing. ... It was around 11:30. We went out on the balcony where you could see little red lights which the neighbors said were projectiles. Thirty or 40 minutes later four helicopters appeared headed toward the Central Barracks. The helicopters were firing all kinds of weapons because you could hear the bursts and explosions were of different intensities. ...
>
> The lights in the neighborhood went out and houses began to burn. It was chaos. People tried to leave their burning homes but found themselves between two fires ... tanks and armored cars and soldiers were advancing on foot, firing. We could hardly believe it. My son was crying, terrified. The best my sister and I could do was try to protect him with our bodies.
>
> With every bomb blast the building shook and windows shattered. At some point I made my way to the kitchen and somehow brought the tanks of propane gas [for cooking] back to the bathroom, which seemed the most sheltered spot, because the gas tanks were exploding in a lot of the apartments as they were hit by bullets.[16]

Another El Chorrillo resident testified that before leaving their apartment the morning after the assault began, he and his family saw "a group

---

16. Testimony received by the Independent Commission of Inquiry from CONADEHUPA, February 28, 1990.

El Chorrillo before the invasion (above) and after (following pages). Photo above: Rafael Olivardía, El Chorrillo War Refugees Committee. Photos of destruction: Anonymous. (They were sold on the street in Panama City.)

Mr. José Zalas stands in the rubble of his home on the spot where his wife Dionisia was killed. Photo: Carl Glenn

of 18 U.S. soldiers coming down the street. We saw them entering each house. We saw the people—the residents—coming out, followed by the soldiers, and then we saw the houses, one by one, go up in smoke. The U.S. soldiers were burning the houses."[17]

The testimonies of the victims tell variations of the same horror story, over and over again. As of this writing, not one of the Panamanians has received compensation or indemnity for the injuries or deaths sustained by them or their families.

Individuals like José Isabel Zalas of Colón and hundreds of others have appealed to the OAS to demand that the United States pay compensation. José's wife, Dionisia Meneses de Zalas, was washing rice for dinner on December 22 when a rocket from a U.S. helicopter smashed into the wood frame building where she and her family lived. Mrs. Zalas was cut in half, her son and daughter injured and left traumatized. The house was a total ruin.[18]

Also appealing to the OAS is Luisa Lee Prado of Colón, whose apartment building was struck by a U.S. missile. As a result of the explosion her daughter lost the vision in her left eye and her 5-year-old son suffered brain damage from a shrapnel wound to the head. These people, low-income workers like most of the civilian victims, have not received a penny of compensation from the U.S. government.

Indiscriminate Violence against Civilians

Operation Just Cause appears to have been implemented with a minimum of what the military euphemistically calls "collateral damage"—that is, civilian casualties and property damage. U.S. soldiers were instructed to fire only at targets posing a direct military threat to them. The use of indirect fires (mortars and artillery) and airstrikes were strictly controlled and could be authorized only by lieutenant colonels and above. ... We heard no complaints from Panamanians about the indiscriminate use of firepower by U.S. troops.

Les Aspin (D-WI), Chair of House Armed Services Committee

Thousands of Panamanians were killed and wounded during the invasion. The bulk of these casualties were civilians. Estimates of the numbers killed range from over 1,000 to as many as 4,000. A precise figure is hard to arrive at because the U.S. government has carried out a deliberate and systematic cover-up of the numbers killed. (This will be covered later in this report.)

---

17. Testimony taken by the first joint delegation of CONADEHUPA and CODEHUCA, January 23, 1990, Case #3.

18. Testimony given to Independent Commission of Inquiry investigator Carl Glenn by Mr. Zalas while standing in the midst of the charred ruins of his home.

The invasion strategy of using disproportionate force and "overkill" continued for weeks, whenever the occupying troops encountered resistance or the *perceived threat* of resistance.

CODEHUCA on April 16, 1990, issued the second of two reports based on the findings of investigating teams sent by the human rights organization to Panama. The CODEHUCA report cites numerous cases of U.S. soldiers' indiscriminate killing of unarmed Panamanian civilians, including air attacks on clearly identified civilian housing, firing on civilian cars at roadblocks, and outright assassinations of Panamanian civilians. CODEHUCA investigators interviewed Panamanian public prosecutor Luis Felipe Muñoz, who told the team that he had received numerous reports of cases of U.S. armed attacks on Panamanian civilians. As an example, Muñoz cites testimony from one such case:

> There was a bus on [December] 27th, on the Trans-Isthmus [Highway] ... on which there were several wounded people on board. Some young men got on the bus to bring them to the hospital, and there was a barricade and several cars stopped behind them. A car came up behind them with Panamanian paramilitaries that fired at the North Americans and then they (the North Americans) fired at all the cars—from the first to the last in line. There in the bus seven died. There was a VW with a pregnant woman and her husband inside. It was an indiscriminate way to shoot, from the front of the line to the back, killing almost all. There were many cases like that. The North Americans put up roadblocks, and the people didn't know anything about them. When they arrived at night, there wasn't much light, and the persons braked at the same time as they were shot.[19]

Another example of the U.S. strategy of placing all the burden and risk onto Panamanian civilians whenever the U.S. invading force felt threatened occurred a week after the invasion. U.S. helicopters circled a residential area in Colón, far from the military bases. When a sniper reportedly fired a shot from a 15-story apartment house, the helicopter launched rockets into that building and several nearby homes (including the house of the Zalas family mentioned earlier).

In another case revealed to CODEHUCA by Public Prosecutor Muñoz, the sister of a civilian killed by U.S. troops and then buried in a common grave in Colón testified:

> We arrived there and found the car where they had been detained by the Americans. All five of the passengers of the vehicle were forced out of the car and put face down on the floor. They were riddled with bullets. It was the 23rd of December. ... They were simply going to visit family

---

19. Testimony taken by the second joint delegation of CONADEHUPA and CODEHUCA and contained in the CODEHUCA Report of April 16, 1990, Document #16.

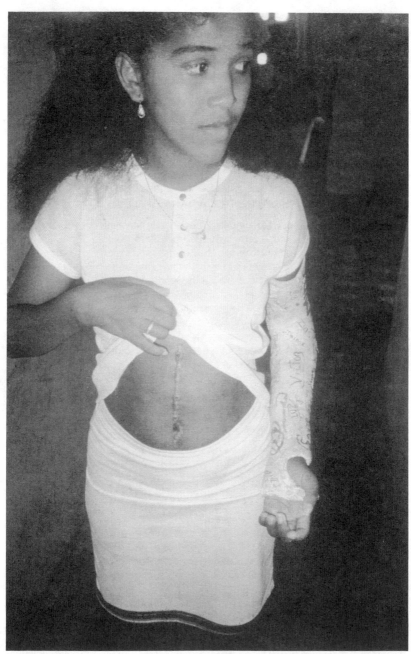

One of five children wounded by shrapnel during the bombardment of a small house in San Miguelito by an attack helicopter. Photo: Carl Glenn

members when they were detained and killed in the street. Witnesses told me that from the ground they begged not to be killed. ... They died in a roadblock on the way to Chilibre. ... The youth who picked them up said they were in a position of surrender, face down with their hands up. ... When they took my brother [from the mass grave], you could see the holes in the back of his sweater. ... Afterwards, they burned the flesh that remained on the road. ... The neighbors saw everything.[20]

Why resort to the wanton killing of civilians? Apologists for the invasion will say, "Civilians die in every war. It's too bad, but it's in the nature of war." But in Panama the widespread death of civilians resulted from the logic of a particular type of war and from a very particular military strategy, one designed to minimize U.S. casualties by maximizing Panamanian casualties.

The U.S. troops faced the same problem confronting all *invading armies,* particularly in a combat situation with no fixed front lines. They found themselves in this sense in a situation parallel to Vietnam, where U.S. troops frequently fired on civilians whom they suspected were giving aid and comfort to the "enemy," or *were* the "enemy."

It is not always so easy to differentiate between a civilian, a member of the Dignity Battalions, a PDF soldier out of uniform, or an individual Panamanian patriot willing to take life-risking actions to protest the occupation of his or her country. This inherent problem facing all invading armies, coupled with the heavy dose of spoon-fed racism and gung-ho military hysteria pushed by the officers corp, sent a clear message about the rules of engagement to U.S. troops: "Shoot first, ask questions later." The Dignity Battalions, who were characterized in the U.S. press only as Noriega's "thugs" and who carried out a good part of the resistance to the invasion, were made up of both blue collar and professional workers, men and women. Considering that they fought against such overwhelming forces, where death in combat was likely and the chances for victory so small, their resistance will undoubtedly be remembered for its heroism by many patriotic Panamanians.

The CODEHUCA delegation interviewed two Panamanian civilians who had been wounded in the following incident, in which two civilians were killed and five others injured:

> On December 20, we were travelling on the Interamerican Highway between La Chorrera and Arraijan in a private car when we were intercepted by a tanker and a "Hummer" vehicle [HMMWV armored jeep] of the U.S. Army. We stopped because we thought that it was a routine check. To our surprise, a grenade or something similar was shot from the tank which

20. Ibid., Document #7A.

Bodies in the morgue at Santo Tomás hospital after the invasion.

killed two people, Rubina González and José Espinosa. ... After firing, the soldiers withdrew.[21]

Contrary to the statements of Representative Aspin and others, the "indiscriminate" and "disproportionate" use of force was common. For example, residential buildings in El Chorrillo and elsewhere were repeatedly attacked by missile and machine-gun fire from Apache helicopters. Representative Charles Rangel (D-NY) has requested that the Pentagon make available the videotapes, taken from the Apaches, that record the attack. As of June 1990, Rangel's request had been denied by Richard Cheney on grounds of "national security."

Based on interviews conducted by the Independent Commission of Inquiry, the Panamanian human rights group CONADEHUPA, and CODEHUCA, a picture emerges that completely contradicts U.S. government assertions that the invasion was a clean, surgical strike which successfully minimized civilian casualties. The following accounts are based on numerous eyewitness testimonies from morgue and hospital workers, relatives of family members killed, and war refugees made homeless by the destruction of their neighborhoods.

Hospital workers told how during the invasion they were not able to go with ambulances or on foot to pick up casualties because U.S. troops were shooting at the ambulances, even though they had clear Red Cross markings.

U.S. troops occupied the hospitals, carrying out searches and arrests preventing medical personnel from treating victims. U.S. troops surrounded hospitals, making wounded people afraid that if they came for treatment they could be identified as PDF or Dignity Battalion combatants. Many died of wounds because of lack of access to medical personnel and medical supplies, and the interference and occupation of the hospitals by U.S. troops.

Most people were brought to hospitals in private vehicles. In the streets and hospitals bodies were lying everywhere. Many people were killed and injured from shrapnel and re-exploding bullets. Many of the dead were brought in with no marks except a single shot fired into one eye, indicating extra-judicial executions. Others with bullet wounds had also been subsequently bayoneted to make sure they were dead.

Tanks flattened cars with people in them, as well as bodies in the streets. Whole shanties were blown apart by mortar fire while their residents were inside. El Chorrillo residents report soldiers collected bodies in plastic bags and transported them elsewhere, thus concealing the number of dead.

Troops went building to building giving little or no warning to residents

---

21. *Opinión Pública*, March 1990.

before calling in mortar fire, automatic weapons or helicopter fire. Even when people tried to get out of the buildings, they were often forced to run back in because troops were shooting randomly at everyone on the streets.

In one 15-story apartment building in El Chorrillo, residents were given two minutes to get out but couldn't because of the building height. They were trapped there for 12 hours while mortar fire pounded the building, killing residents on many floors while others huddled inside the stairwells.

Troops invaded homes, went through and often stole personal possessions, and then burned the buildings down. Casualties in El Chorrillo, including the dead and wounded, were believed to number in the thousands as a result of the fires.

Some 18,000 residents who could get out were forced to take refuge at Balboa High School, according to Rafael Olivardía, president of the El Chorrillo War Refugees Committee, who helped to register people as they entered the school. People reported being treated as concentration camp prisoners. Soldiers arrested some people as they entered the high school, while registering others. The school was surrounded by wire fences and heavily armed troops. Despite a lack of food and sanitary facilities, families were not allowed to leave the school. Days later when they returned to their neighborhoods, many found their homes destroyed.

In the days following the invasion as many as 20,000 people were made homeless. Thousands took refuge with families and friends. Thousands were forced into schools, other public buildings, and refugee camps like the giant Albrook Field airplane hangar. Some 3,000 people became long-term residents in tiny cubicles in the hangar, where they lacked medical care, privacy, sanitary facilities and adequate, decent food.

Thousands Died

The official U.S. version of the number killed during the invasion still stands at 516 Panamanian deaths, including civilian and combatant casualties, and 3,000 wounded. The United States claims 26 GIs died and another 300 were wounded. Reporters were not allowed to visit the wounded for many days, even those U.S. soldiers flown back to the United States for treatment.

The official U.S. story on the casualty count is widely disputed in Panama, especially by human rights organizations that have carried out independent investigations. CODEHUCA believes that at the very least 2,000 Panamanians died during the invasion.[22] As implausible as the official U.S. count seems, it is good to remember that at the time of Ramsey Clark's fact-finding tour to Panama in early January, and prior to the well-publicized charges

_____

22. See CODEHUCA's response to Americas Watch report, page 100 of this book.

that the United States was lying about the figures, the official U.S. version was that only 84 Panamanian civilians had died. That was during the period when the U.S. media accounts of the invasion read like Pentagon press releases. Story after story described the "neat" and "surgical" character of the invasion and almost all comment on casualties referred only to U.S. servicemen who had been killed or wounded.

The careful management of the news did outrage some leading journalists. Helen Thomas, White House correspondent for United Press International (UPI), complained in a January 31 dispatch from Washington, D.C.,

> And there is a question of a news blackout. Neither Americans, nor anyone else, saw the ravages of the first night bombing or the dead or the wounded in the first days of the invasion. The U.S. managed to block such pictures or news reports by inhibiting and frustrating news coverage.

Thomas quotes Patrick J. Sloyan of the Washington office of *Newsday* who described the *de facto* censorship of the news carried out by the government. Sloyan wrote:

From President George Bush's invasion of Panama, there is not a single public photograph, video or eyewitness account of the moments when 23 U.S. servicemen were killed and 265 wounded.

There is, however, a secret record of what was essentially a one-day war that also resulted in a still uncertain number of Panamanian dead and injured. But the Bush Administration has censored it from public viewing.

The U.S. military made video recordings as well as photographs, and Sloyan quotes an army official who saw the combat photographs as saying that "it is really dramatic stuff."

Noting that the U.S. media pool of reporters and camerapeople, who had been taken to Panama by the Pentagon, were locked up for two days and barred from going to the scene of the fighting, Sloyan asserts,

> The delay in getting the journalists to the scene left a void in the coverage of "Operation Just Cause" that enabled the Bush Administration to control the initial, and, often, the most lasting public perception—a flawless feat of arms on an almost bloodless battlefield.

Getting an accurate count of the casualties has been made deliberately difficult because the Southern Command, immediately following the invasion, removed the official registries from Panamanian morgues and hospitals.

The U.S. troops also placed many corpses into mass graves. The Independent Commission of Inquiry has a list of 14 mass graves compiled from a variety of sources by Carl Glenn, an investigator sent to Panama by the Commission. The mass grave sites are reputed to be located at: Jardín de Paz Cemetery, Juan Díaz Cemetery, Tocumen Airport (seven separate sites), Amador Golf Course (Fort Amador), Ancón, Cocolí,

Exhumation of mass grave at Jardín de Paz cemetery in Panama City on April 28, 1990. Photo: Vicky Pelaez

Pacora, Tomasito Río Hato, Corazal, San Miguelito, Chilibre, Balboa Cemetery, Monte Esperanza Cemetery (Colón), and a field in Colón.

Under pressure from grassroots organizations like the Association of the Fallen of December 20, 1989, and CONADEHUPA, the Panamanian government conducted an exhumation on April 28 and May 5, 1990, of a mass grave at Jardín de Paz in Panama City. The exhumation was not conducted by an independent forensic pathologist, but rather by the office of the U.S.-installed Attorney General Rogelio Cruz and the government medical examiner's office. Cruz's office, which has Pentagon and State Department "advisors" assigned to it, agreed to the exhumations under the condition that autopsies would not be performed on the corpses. The government admitted that *124 bodies* were discovered in this one grave.

Doctors at the Santo Tomás Hospital have testified that many of the bodies which passed through the hospital morgue were not registered by U.S. troops, who had taken control of the hospital.

The Independent Commission of Inquiry has received numerous individual testimonies, collected by human rights organizations, of people who witnessed U.S. troops using flamethrowers to incinerate corpses on the streets in the days following the invasion.[23]

Many testimonies collected by CODEHUCA attest to the fact that Red Cross access to El Chorrillo was blocked for several days following the invasion and that in El Chorrillo, and other areas, Panamanian corpses were left to decompose in the streets. Other testimonies report that severely wounded Panamanians were left among the piles of dead in El Chorrillo. All of this makes sense from the point of view of the U.S. command taking no actions, including measures demanded by the Geneva Conventions to collect and care for the wounded, if those actions increased the possibility of U.S. casualties.

Public Prosecutor Muñoz told CODEHUCA investigators that during "the first days, only the military and a few civilians were mobilized. We, as Panamanian authorities, were not allowed to enter the morgues until the 24th, four days later, and already the corpses were putrefied, they already had worms ... they brought them from the street after they had been in the sun for two days."[24]

The obstacles to getting an accurate count of the numbers killed and wounded was stated succinctly by Muñoz:

> There is a lack of information because this is an invasion and the North
> Americans have not given us all the information, and there is not a single

23. "Cremation of bodies at the Comandancia of the PDF," CONADEHUPA report of January 24, 1990, Case #8, reporting on action of December 22, 1989.
24. CODEHUCA report of April 16, 1990, Document #16, page 4.

authority that would put pressure on the North Americans. Instead it is the international community which is pressuring the North Americans to tell the truth about the numbers of dead. ... The Public Forces [Panamanian] could give you information about the amount of dead military, but the North Americans have all their archives.[25]

The problem of the United States confiscating materials and blocking access to information was pointed out in an interview with Eusebio Marchosky, a Panamanian government auditor. Referring to 15,000 boxes of Panamanian government documents seized by U.S. troops and still withheld from the Panamanian government, Marchosky stated, "The U.S. government and the U.S. Army have been doing things that contribute to the obstruction of Panamanian justice."[26]

Refusal of the United States to hand over Panamanian documents is such a flagrant violation of Panamanian sovereignty that the Southern Command high brass were forced to respond to public criticism. General Maxwell Thurman, head of the Southern Command, in an April 15, 1990, breakfast press briefing gave one of those "just because" answers to press queries about the documents. "There's an enormous quantity of documents. We have them under our custodianship, and I'm satisfied with our custodianship."[27]

Although Pentagon generals may feel it is satisfactory to crudely brush aside questions about missing documents, the Bush Administration knew that such a posture was politically dangerous when it came to inquiries about missing people.

In response to growing pressure from the relatives of family members who died or disappeared, the United States helped establish the "Linking Committee," which consisted of the Public Forces (the U.S.-created security force that replaced the demolished PDF), the U.S. Southern Command, Catholic Church, and International Red Cross. The Linking Committee was responsible for responding to public inquiries regarding dead and disappeared family members.

The Linking Committee serves a useful purpose for the Bush Administration, helping to answer the criticism that the United States is engaged in a cover-up about civilian deaths. The Linking Committee does *not,* however, actively investigate reports of dead or disappeared Panamanians, but instead informs family members who make inquiries whether their relatives appear on the Committee's lists of confirmed dead or detained persons.

Although the Linking Committee has not pursued any investigations

---

25. Ibid., page 5.
26. From a UPI dispatch of May 13, 1990.
27. Compuserve's Executive News Service, June 15, 1990.

into the whereabouts of missing people, First Lt. Aguilera de García of the Committee admitted to CODEHUCA investigators that the Linking Committee had received 1,400 reports from families with relatives "missing" since the U.S. invasion. According to Isabel Corro, leader of the Association of the Fallen of December 20, 1989, the International Red Cross had collected between 1,500-1,600 reports of "disappeared" persons.

Sometimes words get used so frequently that they lose their meaning. "Disappeared" is one of those words. As Isabel Corro states, "People don't disappear. They don't mysteriously vanish into thin air. No, they are human beings who have been killed and their bodies dumped unceremoniously into mass graves, or incinerated, or dumped into the sea."[28]

Not surprisingly, fear of retaliation constitutes one of the greatest obstacles to getting a full accounting of the dead. Without any apparent incentive to report the death of a loved one or family member, especially in the early days of the invasion when U.S. troops were routinely arresting anyone slightly suspected of being associated with the Dignity Battalions, families and neighbors reportedly buried the dead on their own. Fear of arousing suspicion among the authorities was great enough that families buried their loved ones in their own back yards, according to a National Lawyers Guild investigating team.[29]

Fear of retaliation was not limited to the poor or those considered to be pro-Noriega. High-ranking government officials were worried too. Public Prosecutor Muñoz told CODEHUCA investigators, "It is possible people are afraid to talk. How am I supposed to know that the information that I'm giving you is not going to get me in trouble."[30]

CODEHUCA and CONADEHUPA estimate that at least 2,000 people died during the invasion. Following his fact-finding tour to Panama, Ramsey Clark said that he felt an accurate number of those killed lay between 1,000-4,000. In a statement issued a few weeks after the invasion, Bishop Emiliani of Darien Province and Bishop Aríz of Colón charged that 3,000 had died as a result of the invasion. Bishop James Ottley, Episcopal Bishop of Panama, also asserted that 3,000 were killed.

The Occupation

As American forces continue to patrol the streets of Colón, a new city council has been formed, a new provincial governor selected, and the city's

---

28. From the testimony of Isabel Corro to a University of Panama human rights seminar on February 28, 1990, recorded by Independent Commission of Inquiry investigator Carl Glenn.

29. *Guild Notes,* publication of the National Lawyers Guild, March/April 1990, Vol. XIV, No. 2.

30. CODEHUCA Report of April 16, 1990, Document #16.

police force is being reorganized. The city of Colón is being reborn under the supervision of American fighting forces.

> Tropic Times, December 27, 1989
> Newspaper of the U.S. Southern Command

The return to old-style colonial rule was openly celebrated by the Pentagon reporters a little more than a week after the invasion. Colonialism, that is, the rule of one country by an unelected foreign occupying power, is by far the least democratic form of governmental rule.

During the invasion U.S. troops carried out the destruction of the offices of almost every political organization and newspaper known to oppose U.S. policy. The U.S. invasion force destroyed Panama's National Radio and another radio station, Sistema Radial De Onda Popular. Two television stations, channels 2 and 5, were also taken over by U.S. troops. The newspaper La República, which reported on the extensive death and destruction caused by the invasion, was ransacked and looted by U.S. troops. La República publisher Escolástico "Fulele" Calvo was arrested and taken by U.S. troops to Fort Clayton. He was held there for six weeks and then moved to the Panama City prison Cárcel Modelo. Calvo was never notified of formal charges during the entire time he was held by U.S. authorities. Many Panamanian journalists were either arrested or fired. According to Euclides Fuentes Arroyo, president of the Journalists Union, the U.S.-installed Endara government had prepared a list of 32 Panamanian journalists who were not allowed to leave the country.

The Independent Commission of Inquiry estimates that as many as 7,000 people were arrested by the invading force. A Southern Command spokesman, Lt. Col. Jerry Murguia, told a press conference that 4,446 Panamanians had been arrested as of December 26, 1990.[31] Many prisoners were kept blindfolded for days.

In Santa Ana, U.S. troops barged into the offices of the Youth Movement of the Kuna Indians, arresting members and destroying the organization's files.

U.S. troops had lists of people to be arrested and were dispatched to the homes of almost all previous government, university, trade union, cultural, and political leaders who had been associated with the cause of Panamanian nationalism since 1968. Prisoners were held at Fort Clayton, Empire Range, and other U.S. military installations. Extensive physical and psychological interrogations were carried out by U.S. military intelligence. Symbolizing the reassertion of colonial "right," prisoners were interrogated by U.S. personnel rather than representatives from the Endara government.

Every public building, ministry and university was placed under the

---

31. Tropic Times, December 27, 1989.

U.S. soldiers guarding entrance to Santo Tomás hospital emergency room in February 1990. Photo: Carl Glenn

control of U.S. troops. U.S. troops patrol the streets of Panama City, Colón, San Miguelito and other areas.

Shortly after the invasion, the Southern Command announced it was carrying out "Operation Promote Liberty." Described by the Pentagon as a "nation-building" plan, Operation Promote Liberty was designed to completely overhaul the former governmental, military and judicial apparatus in Panama. The U.S. government has some experience in "nation-building." In Vietnam in 1956, it set about erecting a whole new government apparatus, creating a "south" Vietnam where no such entity previously existed. The essence of Operation Promote Liberty appears to be a purge by the new state and governmental apparatus of any nationalist or anti-U.S. forces.

Mass firings and arrests in January and February coincided with a campaign of vilification and slander unleashed in the press, which functioned in the first period after the invasion only by the tolerance of U.S. military authorities. Advertisements were taken out in the newspapers asking people to turn in supporters of the former government.

On January 25, five weeks after the U.S. invasion and several weeks after President Bush proclaimed that "Operation Just Cause" had accomplished all its objectives, U.S. troops arrested Dr. Romulo Escobar Bethancourt at his home in Panama City. Why arrest Dr. Bethancourt, a Black Panamanian who is probably Panama's foremost authority on international law?

Bethancourt was the chief negotiator for the Panamanian side in the Panama Canal Treaties of 1977.

The United States held Bethancourt incommunicado for five days at

Fort Clayton. No formal charges were placed against him and he was released after an international campaign had been launched on his behalf. Even days after his arrest, Bethancourt's family was not told where he was being held. His whereabouts were finally learned by the Independent Commission of Inquiry by pressuring the U.S. State Department. It is impossible that the United States felt it could jail someone of Bethancourt's stature for any period of time. More likely his arrest was meant to have a chilling effect on the domestic opposition, that is, to serve notice on all potential opponents to the Endara government that the United States was willing to arrest anyone.

Beginning February 2, the new Panamanian Attorney General, Rogelio Cruz, issued arrest orders for hundreds of former cabinet ministers, heads of agencies, legislators, as well as former presidents Manuel Solís Palma and Francisco Rodríguez. The list included almost all prominent Panamanians associated with the cause of Panamanian independence during the past decades. The accused were charged with a previously unheard of crime, "impeding the powers of the renewal of the state." According to Attorney General Cruz, conviction on this charge carries a penalty of from 5 to 20 years imprisonment and denial of the right to hold public office in the future.

This "legal action" was a particularly crude device to intimidate or crush the leadership of a potential domestic political opposition. The names of the accused were prominently publicized in the newspapers. Then Cruz announced he was staying the arrest order while holding open the option to prosecute in the future.

The U.S. "nation-building" scheme involved more than intimidating or repressing leaders at the top. Green Beret forces from the military's Special Operation Forces (SOF) were employed to carry out a similar function at the grassroots level. This work was discussed in the February 5 issue of *Defense Week,* which interviewed a Green Beret named Simpson and others. Simpson stated that his job was to go around Panama City gathering information from citizens about Dignity Battalion and PDF members. U.S. troops seen escorting Public Forces officers on arrests "provide transportation and muscle." (This is understating the U.S. role; in these "police patrols," one lone Panamanian sits in the back of the jeep while two U.S. soldiers in front direct the operation.) As a sign of real political sensitivity, however, the troops report that in order to reinforce the idea that Panama is still sovereign, they have stopped flying the U.S. flag on patrol vehicles, replacing it with a Panamanian flag.

On June 15, 1990, General Maxwell Thurman, head of the Southern Command and in charge of the invasion, announced that the United States had established a military support group that is "working with the new Panamanian government" to reshape the new Public Forces, with the aim of making sure that the military never becomes an independent power again. The military support group provides "logistical, communication, engineering and other assistance" to the Endara government.[32] The support group is headed by the controversial Col. James J. Steele, who came under congressional scrutiny for his involvement with Oliver North's illegal operation to resupply the Nicaraguan Contras. Steele was in charge of the U.S. Military Assistance Group in El Salvador from 1984-1986, years in which thousands of Salvadorans were killed by the U.S.-backed military.

The Independent Commission of Inquiry obtained a copy of a U.S. Armed Forces flowchart naming U.S. military and State Department officials who have been assigned to 22 Panamanian government ministries and agencies.[33] This flowchart reveals that the United States maintains a shadow government in the Panamanian civilian government. The list names a Brig. General Gann and a Mr. Bushnell of the State Department as the U.S. officials assigned to President Endara's office.

To say that Panama has been recolonized is not just a rhetorical flourish. The following incident, simple as it seems, aptly summarizes the new U.S.-Panamanian relationship. It is based on an interview conducted with a trade unionist by a joint CONADEHUPA-CODEHUCA delegation.[34]

Said the trade unionist:

> On January 17, 1990, we organized a picket line in front of the Presidential residence. This had to do with the massive dismissals that are occurring. President Endara agreed to meet with four of us. Inside the building, we were going up the stairs with Endara, when a U.S. colonel called to us from the top of the stairs, saying, "No one can go upstairs. Go and look for another room." He spoke very good Spanish, but with a U.S. accent. Upon hearing this, Endara turned around and we all went back down. He said to us, "Why don't we sit down in this little room."

The Struggle of the Homeless, Displaced and Unemployed

The invasion and occupation of Panama, coming on the heels of more than two years of economic destabilization, has alarmingly increased the misery and hardship endured by Panama's poor.

---

32. Compuserve's Executive News Service, June 16, 1990.

33. See pp. 50-51.

34. Testimony taken by first joint delegation of CONADEHUPA and CODEHUCA, cited in CODEHUCA Report of January 27, 1990, Document 10.1.

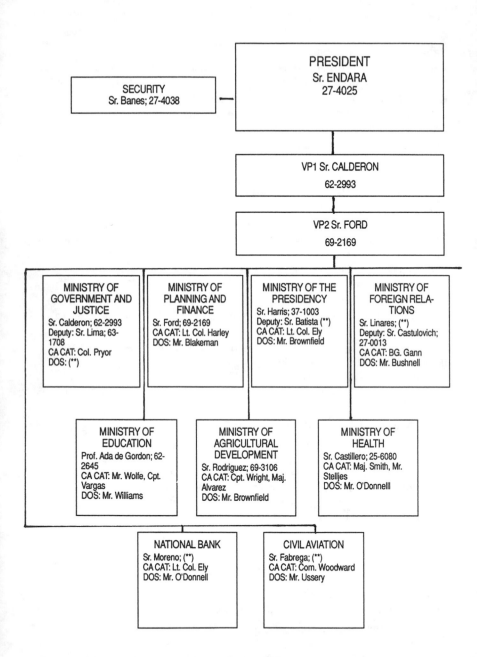

PRESIDENT
Sr. ENDARA
27-4025

SECURITY
Sr. Banes; 27-4038

VP1 Sr. CALDERON
62-2993

VP2 Sr. FORD
69-2169

MINISTRY OF GOVERNMENT AND JUSTICE
Sr. Calderon; 62-2993
Deputy: Sr. Lima; 63-1708
CA CAT: Col. Pryor
DOS: (**)

MINISTRY OF PLANNING AND FINANCE
Sr. Ford; 69-2169
CA CAT: Lt. Col. Harley
DOS: Mr. Blakeman

MINISTRY OF THE PRESIDENCY
Sr. Harris; 37-1003
Deputy: Sr. Batista (**)
CA CAT: Lt. Col. Ely
DOS: Mr. Brownfield

MINISTRY OF FOREIGN RELA-TIONS
Sr. Linares; (**)
Deputy: Sr. Castulovich; 27-0013
CA CAT: BG. Gann
DOS: Mr. Bushnell

MINISTRY OF EDUCATION
Prof. Ada de Gordon; 62-2645
CA CAT: Mr. Wolfe, Cpt. Vargas
DOS: Mr. Williams

MINISTRY OF AGRICULTURAL DEVELOPMENT
Sr. Rodriguez; 69-3106
CA CAT: Cpt. Wright, Maj. Alvarez
DOS: Mr. Brownfield

MINISTRY OF HEALTH
Sr. Castillero; 25-6080
CA CAT: Maj. Smith, Mr. Stelljes
DOS: Mr. O'Donnelll

NATIONAL BANK
Sr. Moreno; (**)
CA CAT: Lt. Col. Ely
DOS: Mr. O'Donnell

CIVIL AVIATION
Sr. Fabrega; (**)
CA CAT: Com. Woodward
DOS: Mr. Ussery

Partial reproduction of U.S. government flowchart showing names of Pentagon and State Department officials assigned to Panamanian functionaries. This document was obtained by the Panamanian resistance.

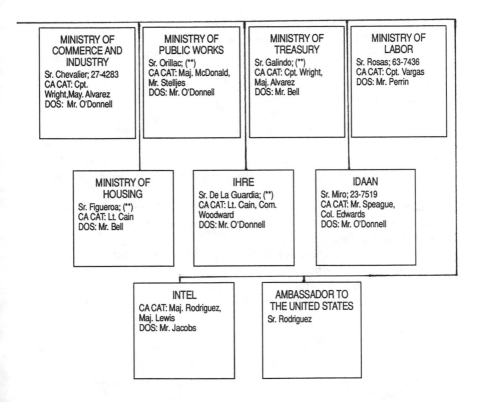

SECRETARY
Sr. Beliz; 37-0013

CA CAT: BG Gann (**)
DOS: Mr. Bushnell (**)

CA CAT: (**)
DOS: 27-1777 (U.S. Embassy)

MINISTRY OF
COMMERCE AND
INDUSTRY
Sr. Chevalier; 27-4283
CA CAT: Cpt.
Wright,May. Alvarez
DOS: Mr. O'Donnell

MINISTRY OF
PUBLIC WORKS
Sr. Orillac; (**)
CA CAT: Maj. McDonald,
Mr. Stelljes
DOS: Mr. O'Donnell

MINISTRY OF
TREASURY
Sr. Galindo; (**)
CA CAT: Cpt. Wright,
Maj. Alvarez
DOS: Mr. Bell

MINISTRY OF
LABOR
Sr. Rosas; 63-7436
CA CAT: Cpt. Vargas
DOS: Mr. Perrin

MINISTRY OF
HOUSING
Sr. Figueroa; (**)
CA CAT: Lt. Cain
DOS: Mr. Bell

IHRE
Sr. De La Guardia; (**)
CA CAT: Lt. Cain, Com.
Woodward
DOS: Mr. O'Donnell

IDAAN
Sr. Miro; 23-7519
CA CAT: Mr. Speague,
Col. Edwards
DOS: Mr. O'Donnell

INTEL
CA CAT: Maj. Rodriguez,
Maj. Lewis
DOS: Mr. Jacobs

AMBASSADOR TO
THE UNITED STATES
Sr. Rodriguez

(**) Illegible.

Unemployment, which had soared to nearly 30% after the imposition of U.S. economic sanctions, has continued to rise. The magazine *Diálogo Social* reports that unemployment in Colón, a mainly Black city, had jumped to 55% as of May 1990.

As many as 20,000 public service workers, and possibly more, lost their jobs after the invasion. FENASEP, the union representing public service workers, attributes the firings to a political witchhunt against politically "unreliable" workers and also to the Endara government's desire to please the International Monetary Fund (IMF), which has been demanding that Panama reduce its public work force. Such summary dismissals of workers were difficult for the government to carry out in the past because of the relatively progressive Labor Codes established in the early 1970s under the Torrijos government. The IMF has also demanded that the Labor Codes be abolished.

Homelessness was dramatically increased by the invasion. Thousands of families had their homes destroyed in El Chorrillo, San Miguelito, Colón and other cities. Exact figures on how many were made homeless are hard to determine. In the early days of the invasion the figures in the U.S. mass media ranged from 15,000-25,000. Some early estimates from Panama put the figure as high as 50,000. As anyone familiar with the homeless situation in the United States knows, counting the homeless is extremely difficult. Those made homeless will try to move in with friends and families. Those who have any resources may stay homeless for a short period until they can find another place to live. Those who live in public shelters are easier to count than those who live literally on the streets or in makeshift shelters.

One week after the invasion, the Southern Command's logistical operation that was dealing with the war refugees ordered food to feed 50,000 people for a seven-day period.[35]

Two months after the invasion the Association of the Missing and other grassroots organizations, representing the displaced from El Chorrillo and other areas, commonly put the figure of homeless at between 13,000-15,000. In mid-March there were still 3,000 people living in the massive hangar at Albrook Field.

The war refugees and the new homeless formed mass organizations that have conducted dramatic actions to win relief from the United States and the Endara government. For those far away from this brutal situation, it is hard to imagine the anger and frustration that grips people whose whole lives are suddenly and without warning uprooted, and who for no reason of their own making are plunged into great suffering. For this reason we quote at length the following letter (dated May 29, 1990) from a

---

35. *Tropic Times,* December 27, 1989.

U.S. soldiers guard the Holiday Inn in Panama City while other units are making poor Panamanians homeless. This photo was one of many showing aspects of the invasion being sold on the streets of Panama.

refugee at Albrook to the New York City Spanish-language daily paper, *El Diario-La Prensa*:

> We refugees are suffering a very severe crisis. Our children are getting sick more and more. They need better nourishment as they give us here three pieces of bread and a cup of tea for breakfast at 7:30 in the morning. That's it until 5:00 p.m. when they serve us macaroni with chicken necks and beans. If for some reason those that work during the day don't get back until 6:00 p.m., this meal is completely missed, and for this reason, many go hungry. When I am overcome by hunger, I eat this meal, but I throw up all night. Mr. Muñoz, to whom we address our complaints, says that we are imagining things. Also, we want to tell you that all of the refugees are entitled to $1.50 food allowance per day. However, for those who do not eat (because it makes them sick), nobody returns this money to them.
>
> Also, we are allotted $500 a month, but they don't give us this money, they give us a book of scrip which is not recognized in any store in the Republic of Panama, with the exception of stores owned by people related to members of the new government.
>
> Another complaint that we, the thousands of families living here, have is the lack of hygiene and the unbearable heat of the refugee camp which is inside a hangar made of galvanized steel. At midday, this is like an oven and we have nowhere to go. When we complain, they call us troublemakers

and the soldiers punish us without even allowing us the right to enter their office. Because of this, the others are afraid to say anything.

Up until today, I still don't know who is going to pay for my property and my car that I used to use for work—they were destroyed by the U.S. soldiers on December 20. I am an assistant mechanic but I'm out of a job. We are starving. I only ask God to give me the strength and health to keep fighting for my family.

José Hidalgo, Albrook Field Refugee Camp, Panama City

Conditions of squalor, homelessness and unemployment sparked a renewal of grassroots struggle, even under the difficult conditions of foreign military occupation. Over 500 El Chorrillo residents living in Albrook occupied the Casa de Piedra apartment building on February 25. The squatters demanded that the building, which was still under construction, be purchased by the U.S. government and handed over to them.

In another dramatic action calling attention to the needs of the war victims, 300 El Chorrillo residents on February 27 took over the Bridge of the Americas, halting all traffic on this key national artery. (The bridge links Panama City on the east bank of the Canal with the rest of the country on the west side of the waterway.)

Vice President Arias Calderón and Housing Minister Raul Figueroa came to the bridge to negotiate with the demonstrators. The El Chorrillo refugees ended their protest only after they were promised a meeting with President Endara and $6,500 (in scrip) for each family.

In early March, 5,000 people in San Miguelito marched against joblessness. They were viciously attacked by the Public Forces, with clubs and dogs. Days later, hundreds of U.S. troops swept into the neighborhood with helicopters and heavy equipment, going door to door questioning and arresting people. The U.S. authorities claimed they were looking for drug dealers.

Invasion Targets the Working Class

At the outset of the invasion of Panama, U.S. troops specifically targeted the labor movement for repression. Leading trade unionists, in both the public and private sectors, were arrested at their homes and dragged off to military prison at Fort Clayton, a U.S. military base.

Some of the leaders arrested included Eric Grael from the National Confederation of Workers of Panama (CNTP); Elías Elías González, Coordinating Committee of Government Unions; Mauro Murillo, CNTP General Secretary; Gustavo Martínez, leader of the Telephone Workers Union (SITINEL); Juvenal Jíminez of the Banana Workers Union; and Aniano Pinzón from the Confederation of Workers of the Republic of Panama (CTRP).

These labor officials were held for three weeks by a foreign occupying force without charges ever being filed against them. During those weeks, U.S. troops occupied government ministry offices and thousands of public service workers were fired. The summary firings of workers, without charges or due process, violated the Panamanian Labor Code which was the law of the land. Did the United States detain Panamanian labor leaders because of their known criminal wrongdoing—or because the Pentagon wanted to leave the workers leaderless while they were spearheading an illegal, anti-labor offensive?

The U.S. public was led to believe that the enemy pursued by the Bush Administration was only Noriega and a handful of "corrupt PDF officers" who constituted his high command. This is one reason for the demonization process against Noriega in the U.S. media—obscuring from working people in the United States that it is people just like them in other countries who are often the targets and victims of U.S. military interventions.

Four of the major trade union confederations—the National Confederation of Workers of Panama (CNTP), the Federation of Public Employees (FENASEP), the Coordinating Committee of Government Unions, and the Confederation of Workers of the Republic of Panama (CTRP)—issued a declaration under the auspices of the Unitary Workers Commission (CUT) shortly after the invasion:

> We, as the working class, will not shirk our responsibilities in the defense of our nation, much less in the defense of workers' rights and of the gains which we have won.
>
> CUT makes a fervent call to all of its affiliates to maintain unity in defense of their class interests and it exhorts their collaboration in the work of reconstructing our job centers and in this way help to maintain the source of employment and at the same time, within the existing reality, to defend the rights and the conquests of the workers.

In the three months following the invasion, conditions for workers and particularly for the organized labor movement gravely deteriorated.

On May 1, 15,000 workers joined a union-led May Day demonstration. The marchers demanded that union rights and Panama's Labor Code be respected. The marchers energetically chanted, "U.S. troops, assassins, OUT!" They also condemned the Endara government as traitorous, illegal and representative of the rich oligarchy.

The workers demanded no privatization of the public sector, particularly the country's main resource, the Panama Canal.

A U.S. trade unionist, Diane Goldberg, Vice President of AFSCME Local 457 in Detroit, delivered a solidarity message to the Panamanian May Day rally. She interviewed scores of union leaders and members during her stay in Panama. Goldberg provides the following account:

Over 100,000 workers have been fired since the U.S. installed the Endara government. Workers are afraid with every bi-weekly paycheck that a pink slip will accompany it; their very participation in the May Day march was a risk to the jobs of those still employed.

The public sector, which includes workers in the formerly state-owned cement, telephone, electricity, and water companies, as well as workers from the public ministries, municipalities and universities, has experienced 12,000 firings so far with another 15,000 expected this year; massive privatization for profit of this sector is accompanying the discharges at the behest of the International Monetary Fund (IMF) and its member banks from the U.S. and other countries.

Nine members of the 15-member executive board of FENASEP have been fired, along with 150 other leaders in the federation. In the construction industry, 95% of the workers, 45,000 in all, are out on the street.

In addition, the government and corporations have abrogated and are seeking to gut the workers' "Código de Trabajo" or Labor Code, a progressive document won during the 1970s which guarantees many rights, including 30 days vacation for all workers after 11 months seniority, maternity rights for women workers, and the right to a job.[36]

U.S. Military Operations May Be Permanent

Two months after the "surgical" military operation was supposed to have accomplished all its objectives, U.S. troops were still carrying out military sweeps, both in the provinces as well as in Panama City.

In late February, U.S. troops swept into the provinces, conducting house-to-house interrogations in Bocas Del Toro, Chiriquí, Veraguas and Darien. According to Carl Glenn, an investigator for the Commission of Inquiry who was in Panama at the time, U.S. soldiers were arresting unionists, community leaders, and directors of farmworkers' organizations and cooperatives in these areas.

U.S. troops were particularly interested in finding out who from the peasant cooperatives had taken part in visits to Nicaragua and Cuba. These trips were organized to give small farmers in Panama's cooperative movement an opportunity to observe the Cuban and Nicaraguan models of agricultural production.

Green Berets and other U.S. forces took control of the jungle area in Darien province along the Colombian border. These troops are now involved in secret military operations against the anti-government guerrilla movement in Colombia. The Revolutionary Armed Forces of Colombia (FARC) and the Colombian National Liberation Army are known to have popular support and bases on the Colombian side of the border.

Information about U.S. military operations in the Colombia/Panama

---

36. *Workers World* newspaper, New York, May 17, 1990.

border region were first reported in the United States by David Adams, an investigative reporter for the San Francisco *Chronicle*. His accounts have been confirmed by local residents, Panamanian officials, and U.S. soldiers.

"Elite [U.S.] Special Forces units patrol the rivers that wind through the dense rain forest ... to the Colombian frontier. The units ... stop local peasants and check documents. Local officials say that some immigrants are being handed over to the U.S. military for questioning," Adams wrote in a May 23, 1990, article. "... The men in the operation reportedly wore 'sterile uniforms' with no identifying patches."

Although officially denying that the United States is conducting military operations in Darien, Colonel Robert Jacobelly, head of the Special Operations Command in Panama, told Adams that the Special Forces were conducting exercises in the area with approval from Washington and the new government in Panama. A Special Forces sergeant interviewed at Yaviza airfield, 30 miles from the border, said: "We were told to expect drugs and [Colombian and Panamanian] guerrillas."

These military operations in Darien support the view that the invasion of Panama is part of a strategy to project U.S. military power, including U.S. combat troops, against revolutionary movements throughout the region. Moreover, four months after the invasion, the U.S. Congress passed a bill allowing the Bush Administration to spend $35 million in the next year to establish Green Beret camps in Peru that will be permitted to carry out military operations against "suspected drug traffickers" and leftist guerrilla movements that have a significant following among poor peasants.

The Drug Connection—of the Endara government

Since General Noriega was indicted for drug trafficking in February 1988 by Miami and Tampa federal grand juries, the Bush Administration and the media have used the drug issue to demonize Noriega in the minds of the U.S. public. Day after day the mass media treated the public to anti-Noriega stories. Looking back at the headlines of the past two years, one can rarely find reference to Noriega without certain adjectives preceding or following his name: "Panamanian dictator," "Panama strongman" or "reputed drug kingpin." All of this had the desired effect of creating a public hysteria and hatred for those targeted as the "enemy."

Long after the invasion, when Panama "vanished" from the media and public attention was directed elsewhere, it was possible for another kind of article to surface. But by then it was harmless. *The New York Times*, which had been in the front row of the anti-Noriega chorus since the

Guillermo Endara, newly installed President, with U.S. troops shortly after the invasion. Photo: El País, Spain

falling out between Reagan and Panama in 1985, printed a front-page story on June 12, 1990, under the headline: "A Thin Paper Trail in Noriega Inquiry—U.S. Finds Few Documents Tying Ex-Leader to Drugs." The article, under the byline of James LeMoyne, begins:

> Despite an unceasing search to find physical evidence of drug dealing by General Manuel Noriega, disappointed American officials say they have found almost no documents so far that conclusively prove General Noriega trafficked in drugs.

So the invasion was carried out despite no real evidence against Noriega?

The article confirms that U.S. authorities seized almost all of Noriega's private and official papers. However, says LeMoyne, the only damaging evidence in the hands of U.S. prosecutors came not from their own research but was given to them by Rogelio Cruz, the new Attorney General in Panama. Cruz provided U.S. investigators with a letter purportedly to Noriega from convicted American drug dealer Steven Kalish. The letter is 16 pages long, written in English and starts with the salutation, "Dear Tony."

What an interesting coincidence that the most "damaging evidence" comes from Cruz. Who is Cruz? Cruz is the former director of the First Interamericas Bank. According to an Oakland *Tribune* editorial of January 5, 1990, the "bank was owned by the notorious leader of Colombia's Cali [drug] cartel, Gilberto Rodríguez Orejuela. It reportedly also laundered money for the Medellín cartel's Jorge Ochoa. At Washington's request,

Panamanian authorities shut down the bank in March 1985."

It is worth mentioning that it is Cruz who keeps Escolástico "Fuele" Calvo, publisher of *La República* newspaper, in jail six months after U.S. troops ransacked and closed his newspaper. *La República* told of Cruz's connection to the First Interamericas Bank in a 1988 article. Calvo's health is deteriorating in prison. He suffers from several life-threatening conditions, including diverticulitis, diabetes and a prostate condition. He was rushed to the hospital from prison for prostate surgery, then returned to jail the next day against doctors' orders. Calvo's friends and family believe that Panamanian officials hope he won't survive the ordeal.

Cruz is not the only Endara government official with possible drug connections. Nearly every senior member of the government, including President Endara, were directors of banks that are considered notorious drug money launderers. Endara, a wealthy corporate lawyer, represented several companies run by Carlos Eleta. *The New York Times*[37] reported that Eleta handled the payoffs of at least $10 million from the CIA to the Endara-led opposition in the May 1989 presidential election. Eleta was later arrested in Georgia on conspiracy to import massive amounts of cocaine into the United States. (All charges were dismissed after the invasion.)

Endara's first ambassador to the United States co-founded the Dadeland Bank in Miami with Vice President Guillermo "Billy" Ford. It was reported that the "bank became notorious several years ago when a Panamanian drug money launderer and co-owner of the bank, Steven Samos, testified that he had used the bank to move vast sums of cash on behalf of a major marijuana smuggler."[38] The Medellín cartel's top money man, Gonzalo Mora Jr., also deposited money in the bank. Steven Samos provided campaign contributions to the present mayor of Panama City, Guillermo Cochez. In 1987, Cochez protested the actions by the Noriega government freezing drug-linked bank accounts.

While it is hard to know exactly who is involved in international drug trafficking, the evidence suggests that the U.S. government and mass media have just as much, if not more, information linking senior leaders in the Endara government to drugs as they did implicating Noriega. The difference in treatment accorded to the Endara government compared to Noriega proves that the drug issue was a ruse masking the larger foreign policy goals the Bush Administration expected to achieve by overthrowing Noriega.

---

37. "Drug Arrests Disrupt CIA Operation," *The New York Times,* January 14, 1990.
38. The Oakland *Tribune,* January 22, 1990.

The Bush Aid Package: Who Gets It?

There is a public perception here, one cultivated by the Bush Administration, that the United States is sending Panama a huge amount of financial aid that will allow Panamanians to recover what they lost during the invasion. A look at the $420 million aid bill signed by Bush in May 1990[39] reveals that those most victimized by both the economic sanctions and the invasion will receive little compensation for their suffering.

One-fourth of the money, $108 million, goes to "reactivate the banking system and increase credit" to private corporations.

Another $244 million, or 58%, is for "a multidonor effort to eliminate Panama's foreign debt arrearages" and support Panama's "public sector investment program." Eliminating Panama's foreign debt arrearages will get the lion's share, $130 million, of the $244 million. This money will go to big foreign banks, principally U.S. banks, who are owed interest payments on Panama's debt, which has increased to a staggering sum for a small country—almost $4.5 billion. A primary reason the interest owed is so great is that Panama has been unable to make any debt payments since the economic contraction caused by U.S. sanctions.

The second part of this section, investment in Panama's public sector, has a promising sound for the possible creation of jobs and services. But it is more likely that these monies will be used in an effort to privatize Panama's public or nationalized economic sector. The United States, the IMF and the World Bank made the privatization of the public sector an important demand on the previous Panamanian government.

The third section of the bill earmarks $68 million for "activities involving natural resources conservation, administration of justice, private sector training, public administration, Peace Corps support and others." How does this actually break down? $12 million will be for police training; $17 million will be for restructuring the nation's judiciary and government apparatus; $10 million will be for Panama Canal improvements (this is the provision called "natural resources conservation"); $7 million will go to human resource development, which includes scholarship and educational grants likely to go to the sons and daughters of Panama's oligarchy and business class; $1.5 million is for Democratic Initiatives, which includes funds for the office of the president and the electoral tribunal and training for a new generation of journalists (remember that the leaders of the Journalists' Union were fired and/or blacklisted because of their opposition to the invasion or because of their nationalist stance); $3 million for export promotion; *only $3 million for housing;* and

---

39. PL-101-302, signed into law by President Bush on May 26, 1990.

$13.4 million for various other projects. These last include police training, cultural exchanges, housing and a vague category called labor development, which could mean that the United States would like to create or support pro-U.S. labor unions to undermine the influence of the anti-imperialist unions that are helping to lead the opposition to the Endara government. Creating nonmilitant and pro-U.S. labor unions has been a standard part of U.S. foreign policy since the end of the Second World War.

Some in Panama might have thought that the invasion would lead to some level of economic relief or even prosperity. Certainly this is an illusion that the U.S. government helped foster. But the Bush aid plan represents a cruel shattering of this idea.

Voices from Panama

Presentations given at the
Town Hall meeting
of April 5, 1990

A Crime Against Humanity

*Speech by Olga Mejía, President of the
National Human Rights Commission of
Panama (CONADEHUPA). Translated from
the Spanish by the Independent
Commission of Inquiry.*

In the name of Gregory Brown, a six-year-old Black child who is buried
in a plastic bag in a common grave in the Mount Hope Cemetery in Colón;
of the daughter of my godmother Mercedes Herrera, a mother of three,
who was machine-gunned to death in Chorrillo; of the soldiers Sidney
Lions and Alejandro Hubart, crushed by North American tanks; of Braulio
Bethancourt, missing since December 20, despite the testimony of
witnesses who saw him being held at the Corte Culebra concentration
camp; of all the Panamanians who gave their lives defending the fatherland against occupation, and the innocent and defenseless victims who
were massacred in El Chorrillo, San Miguelito, Colón, Tocumen, Pacora
and other marginalized communities of Panama:

Accept a most fraternal embrace on behalf of the children, the youth,
the women, the fathers and above all, from all of the mothers who know
what life is and know what it is to lose their most precious loved ones.

The U.S. invasion of Panama perpetrated by the 82nd Airborne Divi-
sion under the U.S. Southern Command, carrying out orders of President
George Bush, is an act of genocide, qualifying as a crime against humanity
and a violation of the sacred right to life, as affirmed by the Universal
Declaration of Human Rights and the internationally recognized Geneva
Accords as well as all the international agreements and enabling protocols
that spell out the most basic norms of international coexistence. Just as in
Grenada and Vietnam, this was never a "Just Cause."

One hundred days after the invasion, the occupying army continues to
operate with impunity and the high cost in human life still remains to be
brought to light. Violence, brutality and the abuse of power that cannot

even be classified as unconventional warfare are used against the civilian, noncombatant population resulting in death, material losses, physical and psychological trauma, and injury to the integrity of the so-called prisoners of war. Arbitrary and illegal searches and seizures are committed by U.S. soldiers.

Panama has been brought into the era of common graves, disappeared people, war refugees and the ransacking of homes. An independent nation has been forced into submission by a colonizing army.

Chorrillo was a marginalized community of some 20,000 inhabitants. Five entire blocks were bombarded; 25th, 26th and 27th streets where I was born and spent my early childhood were completely wiped out and converted into a graveyard. At 12:30 a.m.—in the middle of the night—the bombardment, the strafing and machine-gunning, the firing of rockets began. Later came the use of flame-throwers, tanks and the collective mourning.

They began with the bombardment of the Military Headquarters and then with the massacre of the civilian population. They machine-gunned wood-frame and plaster houses. The interiors of the buildings showed evidence of the use of high-caliber and high-power weapons used against the population as they slept in their beds just days before Christmas. The buildings shook, the residents tried somehow to keep the kitchen propane gas tanks from exploding by bringing them into the bathrooms. The windows were shattered. The walls were filled with holes. The people ran huddled from room to room trying to protect themselves from the hail of bullets.

When the fire started, those who tried to get down using the elevators could not because the power had been cut. Many stayed during the early hours of the morning clinging to each other, hugging the walls of the buildings and risked being burned to death or asphyxiated by the smoke.

Many who ran out trying to flee from the fire and the bombardment died in the streets, machine-gunned by U.S. troops. Others were burned to death in their homes or killed as their homes were bombed. Dawn found many dead in the hallways of their buildings, buried under the rubble or dismembered and totally unrecognizable, either from the bombs and the flame-throwers, or because their bodies were charred or incinerated by the U.S. troops and thrown into plastic bags along with their identification and personal effects. Afterwards, the soldiers threw some of the bodies into the sea. Others were buried in common graves or right where they were found in Chorrillo.

The people who witnessed the charring and cremation of bodies were prevented from attempting to identify the dead. When the people of Chorrillo tried to stop to identify the bodies that lay in the streets, they were forced to move on.

Some bodies were completely destroyed as they were run over by tanks. Some were found at dawn inside of cars, charred or completely crushed by tanks. Hundreds of body parts and fragments of human remains were stuck to the walls of the houses and buildings; they were thrown into plastic bags to which U.S. troops added chemical substances, or they were simply treated as garbage and removed by the backhoes when they cleared away the rubble two weeks later.

There were bodies in the streets of El Chorrillo for nearly a week. The Red Cross was not permitted to recover bodies of either the wounded or the dead to transport them to the hospitals or the morgues. The U.S. troops also opened fire on the ambulances.

The families of the dead were not told whether the bodies of their loved ones had been recovered or where the remains were. There were cases in which families were finally able to locate the bodies of their loved ones two weeks later in common graves but the discovery was by accident as the location of the body did not correspond to where they had supposedly been buried.

There is the case of a student at the Polytechnic Institute, Elizabeth Ramos Rudas, who went to Santo Tomás Hospital to visit her sister who had just given birth, and whose body inexplicably turned up days later in a common grave.

It is for this reason that the massacre against Chorrillo and against Panama must not be permitted to spread throughout Central America and the Caribbean, nor to any other brother country. That is why when we are asked by the giant networks where the 2,000 to 4,000 bodies are buried, we first tell them they should have come to Panama to give a Christian burial to the pieces of flesh and the gallons of blood stuck to the walls of the buildings, or to the unidentifiable human fragments.

Three months after the invasion, we still don't know the precise human toll. Figures range between the official number of 655 to 4,000. The Independent Commission of Inquiry headed by former Attorney General Ramsey Clark estimated the number at between 1,000 and 4,000. The Vicariate of Darien, Kuna Yala and Colón, together with the U.S. Episcopal Conference, speak of 3,000 and condemn the difficulties in obtaining information. The Catholic Church maintains that according to a confidential and creditable source the toll is 655 dead and 2,000 wounded, but they exclude from this count those who burned to death, were cremated, crushed under the rubble, those brought to Gorgas Hospital, those buried in common graves, and all information from the interior. How many do these exceptions exclude?

The Red Cross, cited in *La Prensa*, January 25, 1990, page 12A, mentions 1,463 lawsuits brought by families of people missing since the

20th of December. Of these, 1,249 were declared dead, which means that the rest, 214, are missing.

In reality, the exact figure is not important. What is important is that they are human beings, our compatriots, and we demand to know who they are and where they are.

If it is true that there were only the 655 declared dead by the Southern Command, the Catholic Church and the Endara government, why do these data constitute classified information? Why the mystery surrounding the events at the [Panamanian] Naval Base at Colón? Only 11 of the 145 on duty there at the time of the invasion later turned up alive. Officially only 40 were declared dead. The information from the funeral homes and the situation at the Mount Hope burial site is completely bewildering.

In San Miguelito, Tocumen, Chepo, Chorrera and other population centers affected, nothing is known. A curtain of silence has been drawn around the "accidental" deaths at the roadblocks and those killed during the hours of the curfew. There is complete silence surrounding the circumstances of the mass graves. These exist in the Jardín de Paz, in Corazal and there are accounts of many others—Amador, Balboa, Ancón, Tocumen, San Miguelito. These remain to be investigated.

Many other violations have been committed since the invasion/occupation of December 20 which we will only mention in passing:

Extra-judicial executions, the abuse of power, violence, the use of chemicals and experimental and nonconventional war technology (such as the Stealth F-117A bomber which dropped two 1,000-pound bombs on the Military Academy at Río Hato, laser beams, Hercules C-150s and C-141s, A-37s, Dragonflys, supersonic SR-37s, etc.; some of these weapons were tested for the first time as if these were mere military exercises), the piling up of and the summary execution of the wounded and the burial of bodies together with their identification and identifying personal effects; 6,000 arbitrary and illegal arrests.

Then, there are the material losses. Eighteen thousand war refugees of El Chorrillo demonstrated peacefully to demand housing—and were spat upon. They were thrown out of the schools where they had sought refuge. The living conditions of the refugees in the former airplane hangar at Albrook are not in the least favorable, especially for the children, who have suffered disease epidemics. There are homeless at the Community Board of Santa Ana. In Colón there are more than 200 homeless.

In addition there are the family members of the fallen. Who, when and how will these civilian noncombatants who suffered as a result of the invasion be compensated?

In addition, there is the loss of autonomy and independence in the governing of the country. How will this be rectified?

The United Nations, human rights and humanitarian groups, organizations of jurists, investigators and international tribunals must demand tirelessly:

First, that El Chorrillo, Colón, San Miguelito, Río Hato, etc., be recognized as the Lidices[1] of Central America, so that the atrocities committed against Panama during the invasion and occupation will never again be repeated anywhere on the planet.

Second, that international organizations with expertise in the field of forensic anthropology[2] be granted complete independence and all of the resources necessary to scientifically establish the number, identity and cause of death of those massacred in Panama.

Third, the immediate withdrawal of the U.S. Southern Command and its headquarters and the recognition of the autonomy of the Endara administration.

Fourth, an immediate end to the menace of political persecution against public employees, against members of the former government, against the citizens who belonged to the Dignity Battalions (Article 306 of the National Constitution of Panama), unless their presumed guilt first be proven in a fair and impartial trial with full guarantees of due process.

Finally, with a strong embrace from all the "Voices from Panama," we would like to express our gratitude for your presence because it shows that your hearts and your readiness are with the struggle against the unjust military invasion/occupation of Panama.

---

1. Lidice was a coal-mining town in Czechoslovakia totally destroyed by the Nazis during World War II in reprisal for the execution of Commander Reinhard Heydrich by Czech partisans.

2. Forensic anthropology is a new discipline developed to study cadavers and skeletal remains; it first arose as a product of the many assassinations committed by government death squads in Argentina and Chile.

Edilma Icaza

I Want to Relive
the Invasion with You

*Speech by Edilma Icaza, representative of
the Indigenous Peoples of Panama.
Translated from the Spanish by the
Independent Commission of Inquiry.*

I want to congratulate the members of the Commission who have worked
so hard to bring us here from Panama.

Tonight I want to relive the night of December 20, the invasion, with
you.

At 1 a.m. one of my children woke me up, he knocked on the door
and said, "Mama, they invaded Panama." I went out into the street to fight.

In the name of my dead Native brothers, in the name of my orphaned
brothers, my brothers left homeless, I want to cry out. Tonight I want to
convey the pain I feel as a result of what happened on December 20.

In the name of a brother who was killed on Fourth of July Avenue, the
compañero fell right in front of me. I went back to National Radio and we
continued working with the international radios, until 5 in the afternoon
when the North Americans invaded and took over the station where we
were broadcasting. They took us away, myself and three other women I
was working with there. I can't say any more, I feel overcome by these
recollections. In Panama, the mourning continues.

The North Americans also invaded the Native communities. In the
mountains of the Guaymí, they also came to my village which is called
Justupo on December 30. They destroyed our school, the movie house,
the windows.

I want to tell you, I used to have a job. They fired me on January 1.
They fired my husband, my eldest son and my daughter because they said
we were part of the previous government.

Tonight, compañeros, I feel very emotional describing all that we lived

70

through on December 20, the day of the invasion. Brothers and sisters, we are still fighting. It's not going to stay like this, brothers and sisters.

In the name of my dead brothers and sisters, we must carry on this fight together. Here tonight, you have showed your solidarity and I feel very moved because so many people came here to show their support.

The North Americans think that they own Panama. We are the owners, the Indigenous people are the owners of America. Compañeros, tonight I am remembering all of the fallen brothers and sisters. After, on December 24, I returned to my house in San Miguelito, and I saw that my neighbors who belonged to the Dignity Battalions were not in their homes, that they were in hiding, moving from house to house, because they were afraid that the government would arrest them.

The people fought; they fought in the streets as members of the Dignity Battalions. We have to say that the Dignity Battalions fought in the streets, it was a people's fight. Women were also in the streets fighting.

At this moment I can't remember all of the things I wanted to tell you, but I feel like I want to cry out and say, "Brothers and sisters, we will fight together, until victory we will keep on fighting."

The Workers in Our Country
Are Suffering Great Repression

*Speech by Héctor Alemán, General
Secretary, National Federation of Civil
Service Employees (FENASEP). Translated
from the Spanish by the Independent
Commission of Inquiry.*

It falls to me to report to you about what happened to the workers in
Panama as a result of the invasion. It is important that you know that long
before the invasion the workers had been waging an intense struggle as a
result of the many forms of U.S. aggression against our economy.

As a result of this aggression, in less than two years 250,000 Panamanian workers have lost their jobs. In a country such as ours with a
population of barely 2 million people, this meant that during that period,
unemployment had gone up from 11% to 20%. Now, after the invasion,
according to figures provided by the present government, 35% of the
workers are unemployed.

We know that the actual numbers are higher. In my city, Colón, nearly
55% of the workers are unemployed. Massive unemployment has been
part of a deliberate program of George Bush for the workers in our country.

Among the public employees, the workers represented by my union,
during the last three months more than 12,000 workers have lost their
jobs. The two fundamental reasons for this massive unemployment are
first, the profound political persecution against all of us who opposed and
still oppose this invasion, and secondly, the occupation government is
implementing the measures called for by the International Monetary
Fund, which include the complete privatization of state-owned businesses
and the preparation of a base of operations for transnational corporations
in our society.

The workers and their leaders in our country are suffering great repression. At this moment, the majority of leaders in my union have been fired without any justification whatsoever. Nine members of the National Executive Board of FENASEP have been fired.

These firings are in violation of the fundamental rights of the workers. In addition, they do not recognize any of the benefits of the workers, they do not respect vacation rights, the workers are not receiving pay for days already worked, and even worse, they are violating the rights of women on maternity leaves. That is to say, women workers who were pregnant or on maternity leave were summarily and mercilessly fired.

The leaders of the trade union movement in Panama have been denied the right to carry out our responsibilities, especially with respect to having access to the media. On the contrary, the media has unleashed a campaign against our leaders in order to completely eliminate any possibility that we might be able to continue to struggle.

This persecution also includes closing down our union offices and prohibiting us from speaking with fellow workers whom we represent on the job.

This is the democracy that the invasion brought to our country.

I want to say in the name of my fellow workers in my country; of those who were doubly massacred—who lost their jobs before the invasion and were then murdered during the military assault; and those of us who survived the invasion but today are subject to persecution:

We ask the North American people, the working people of this country, to take on the responsibility today to make the truth about Panama known and understood by all the people of the United States.

Today, it is essential for us that this commitment be fulfilled, because in that way you will be able to really help us so that, from within Panama, independently of the invasion, in the year 2000 the workers and the people of Panama can force the U.S. government to carry out the Canal Treaties and guarantee the liberation of our country.

Please be assured that we will continue to fight and that every day that struggle will be stronger, with greater unity and greater power.

In the name of all the workers in my country, I want to express gratitude to all of you for your presence here tonight. There are many things I would like to share with you tonight, but I hope that I have been able to convey the main points of how the Panamanian workers feel, what they are going through at this moment, because that is what the people should know.

¡Hasta la victoria siempre!

The Panama Case
Has Just Been Opened

*Speech by Mario Rognoni, Former Minister
of Commerce and Industry and presently
opposition leader in the Panamanian
National Assembly.*

I am very grateful to be here tonight because I have regained the hope that we have lost in the United States. Because the United States is not the government, is not what you call the establishment. The United States is the people who live here, the people who elect those officers into governmental positions. The problem is that for some reason, once they get into office, either they lie to the people, they deceive the people, or simply the people don't care what they are doing in the government.

We have been through the worst case of stress between the two countries in our relationship. But it has been quite an experience and I feel that both nations have many things to learn from it. The most important thing to us, at least, is that the people of the United States have to somehow learn to be able to keep track of what the government is doing. As much as you keep track of taxes and domestic problems and domestic issues. Foreign policy is an important part of what the United States government does, and it affects every one of you, one way or another.

The last two U.S. Administrations lied to the American people with great skill. It was very hard for us Panamanians to understand why the U.S. government all of a sudden strangled our economy, went after us like we were criminals, brought us to the point where our gross national product decreased 27%, where we lost more than 20% in per capita income, where they put sanctions, claiming we were a risk to North American security.

We're smaller than Delaware. Our armed forces were smaller than the New York City Police Department. And we were a threat to the United States!

74

And they did everything, including banning the members of government from coming to the United States. They wouldn't let us talk here, they wouldn't let us come to the campuses of the universities, they wouldn't let us present our truth. Instead, they presented the truth that they felt suited their best interests. But in time, history at least gives us that break, in time the truth comes out.

They complained that our country was being run by a drug Mafia. And after the invasion, once they caught everybody they wanted to catch, who do they have involved in drug trafficking? One general, one lieutenant-colonel, two pilots and one civilian. That was the threat to the United States! One of the pilots is already out on bail, and the other is going to get three years in jail. But for that, we lost thousands of lives, we lost a billion dollars in assets, our economy is a shambles.

It is hard to understand how the American people couldn't see through what the government was telling them, a government that has lied on every issue of foreign policy in Central America. They lied on El Salvador, they lied on Nicaragua, they lied with Iran-contra, they lied with Panama, but we knew the truth.

The media played second fiddle to that Administration and would never let it out, because the truth is that the establishment at one point decided to renege on the treaty. They decided that they need the military bases past the year 2000. They decided that the PDF [Panama Defense Forces] which they had trained, armed and given us had become too nationalistic, too independent. And they needed a more submissive one.

So they didn't go to Panama on December 20 to capture one man, as they have claimed. They went out to destroy every military installation we had. They went out and took back the four bases they had given us through the treaties. Right now Cimarron is back in U.S. Army hands. Río Hato is back in U.S. Army hands. Every base they wanted they got back, including the School of the Americas. They took it back, forgetting about the treaties.

Let me tell you something. The image that we had of the U.S. Army is gone. Now the image we have is another. There were looters, there were thieves, there were mercenaries. They killed the wounded because we didn't have enough hospitals and neither did they. That's the only reason they killed them.

They buried our dead in common graves because they were ashamed of what they were doing, but at the same time they were looting. Every time they went into a house, they took the jewelry, the silverware, the money. That they don't say.

They were so nervous, I saw them pointing at a 4-year-old girl with a machinegun. To hold her still. The girl didn't understand English, didn't even understand the gun. That's the army that some of those generals are now praising for the efficiency with which they took over Panama. And for what?

They swore in our new government on a military base in front of an American flag. How can that government have any respect for itself or from anybody?

The day they swore in the government, they gave him [Endara] the list of what he had to do, including putting the relationship with Cuba under stress, stressing the relation with nations with whom we have been friends for years. Now to suit American interests we have to break relations with them. Now they don't want us to have relations with Libya, with Cuba. They allow Nicaragua because Mrs. Chamorro won. Otherwise, it would have been on the list.

The first thing they did in the first week was close eight radio stations, two television stations, four newspapers. This was the democracy that the U.S. Army was backing. We have a democracy where 599 of our political figures now have indictments against them and are subject to go to jail, accused of nothing, simply because they were in the government prior to the invasion.

Everybody who was holding a public office is now accused of "abuse of power," something they came up with to have everybody under the same net.

This is the democracy that we are getting.

We want to make clear that we believe that nations need time to develop their own political systems. The United States took over 200 years to get to where they are. You went through slavery, you went through women without the vote, you went through assassinations of presidents, you went through everything getting here. You cannot expect another country simply to draft a constitution and apply it. You have to grow into that. Our people have to grow into the political system that best fits us. And when we get that democracy, we will cherish it because it's ours. It hasn't been imposed, it hasn't been forced.

It has been a long night and I want to finish by trying to get a commitment from you, because even though the U.S. government has sold the idea that the Panama case is closed, it is exactly the opposite. The Panama case has just been opened.

And the government of the United States now will try, as Panama fades away on the screen of news, to put the real squeeze on Panama, on what they want from us.

They want to destroy the banking center, they want to destroy our service economy, but more important they want to make sure they get a treaty for military bases past the year 2000. And they want to make sure they get the canal administration past the year 2000.

We cannot make this fight alone. The U.S. government already learned a lesson when they fought against General Torrijos and found he had the whole world behind him. They are going to avoid that. So we need the American people to understand our cause, to understand what we are fighting for, to understand our rights and be at least committed to help us be able to stand as a proud nation, to be able to regain our full sovereignty and be an independent state as we should be.

We have now against us not only the strength of the U.S. government but the presence of military troops in Panama in excess of what the treaties allow.

We feel that for the best interests of both nations, the U.S. troops have to be immediately removed from Panama.

Second, the U.S. government has to clearly state its commitment to comply with the Canal Treaties.

Third, the U.S. government must stop intervening in the internal affairs of our country.

That is our cause. We believe in democracy. We feel we can work together among Panamanians in search of the best political structure to really develop our country. But we will not be able to do it as long as we have the overpowering presence of the North Americans within our shores.

I simply want to tell you that even though we are a small country, we are very proud of it. And even though the media sold the idea that the Panamanian people cheered the invasion, and that the Panamanians were happy with what happened, we weren't. There were very few who were cheering, and they were mainly foreigners in some areas. They weren't even Panamanians.

We Panamanians know one thing. We were facing the strongest army in the land, we were facing a power that we didn't even know existed. We were attacked by the highly sophisticated modern technology of warfare. We never expected it.

But we are not down and out. We simply lost the first round. And we will be back.

Graciela Dixon

The People Have Been Pushed into Concentration Camps

Speech by Graciela Dixon, attorney for the El Chorrillo refugees.

Brothers and sisters, because of my West Indian heritage, I will do my best to deliver in English.

Martin Luther King had a dream of peace, of unity, of justice and human rights. On the 20th of December 1989, the Panamanian people also had a dream, the dream of Christmas coming. The Panamanian people also had the dream of freedom for their country. But that dream became a nightmare.

It became a nightmare when 2,000-pound bombs fell over their heads, in their homes, and caught many of them sleeping. They were killed in the most devastating, cruel, inhuman attack from the most powerful armed forces of the world, the U.S. forces.

However, the U.S. establishment has said to the world that they entered into our country to save the people of Panama, to install democracy in Panama. They call this massacre that killed over 4,000 civilians, innocent people, children, women and men, they call it "Just Cause." Now I ask you, how can this criminal act be called "Just Cause"?

Can it be considered a just cause when the United States, the most powerful armed forces of the world, exercised new war techniques against our people, using the most modern inventions to destroy human life? Is it just to kill an innocent child of five years old? Can it be considered just to destroy the people's homes, the workers' homes, to throw them into concentration camps, and then submit them to the most inhuman isolation and reduction of all their rights as human beings?

The Department of Defense described the action against Panama as the largest military action the United States has been involved in since the Vietnam war. Now, you know what the Vietnam war was. We also know.

Why make such comparisons? That comparison is because in Panama they did exactly the same thing in a short time that they did in the Vietnam war.

And the voices of Panama are here tonight not only to put before you the truth about what happened in Panama, but we are here to ask you, perhaps we are here to *demand* from you, a human, civilized behavior, for you to fight together with us, for you to fight the U.S. establishment, for you to insist that the U.S. government take their hands and their feet out of Panama.

We know that all of you may have a question. This question arises from the propaganda in the U.S. establishment-controlled media. I know your question will be, how come the people of Panama applauded the invasion? It was presented to you that way, but the truth hasn't been said.

I must be honest to you and to the world. Yes, there were so-called Panamanians who applauded the invasion, who were happy to see the troops in our streets, who told the soldiers welcome. But those so-called Panamanians who said welcome didn't live in El Chorrillo, didn't live in San Miguelito, or in Colón, my home town, or in Río Hato. Those people who welcomed the soldiers are from the rich, the ruling class in Panama.

But we are here today to tell you what the people from Chorrillo think. How they feel today when they are pushed into concentration camps, when they have to present an ID card signed by the commander-in-chief of the Southern Command, General Marc Cisneros. I want you to know how they feel when they no longer have their yucca and their codfish, but have been forced onto an unsolicited diet of military rations. And they are having that only twice a day.

The official Panamanian governmental commission for human rights stated that the children in the condition of war refugees in those concentration camps are receiving the right meals, according to the Geneva Convention. This proper meal indicates that for breakfast children should have milk, eggs, bread, butter. Do you have the slightest idea what the children in those concentration camps have for breakfast, whenever the breakfast is reached? It is cold coffee and a dry piece of bread. And whoever is not in at 9 has no opportunity to have breakfast. There is no more food until 4 in the evening. Now you tell me if this isn't a poor diet.

At 4 in the evening they get rotten food, cold food. What I'm saying here was announced on the television news in Panama City after a lot of struggle. And what I'm saying has been testified to me as the legal representative of the war refugees in Panama.

The people pushed into these concentration camps are suffering today. They have no privacy. They don't have a chance even to go to the bathroom, and I mention a bathroom not to describe that place. There is no bathroom. They have not even the most elemental condition to sleep, to raise their children.

They have been thrown out of their jobs. Their homes have been destroyed. They no longer have personal belongings. They have been pushed into this forced diet that I just described to you. And on top of that it is prohibited to receive any visitors at their new home, the concentration camp.

If you try to go there, you'll have no opportunity to enter if you don't have that ID card signed by Marc Cisneros.

We will be seeking and demanding support here and worldwide because we have a commitment, and our commitment is to be free. Our commitment is to be a sovereign nation. Our commitment is to control our main reasource, which is the canal, in the year 2000.

Alberto Barrow

Racism Was Central to the Invasion

*Speech by Alberto Barrow of the
Panamanian Black Congress.*

Tonight I appear before you as a Black voice from Panama. You may ask why? I would answer right up front. The U.S. invasion of Panama took the lives of over 4,000 fellow citizens. All of them precious lives. And in addition to that human condition, most of them were Black and Mestizos.

I beg you to bear with me as a Black voice because as a Panamanian of African ancestry I experience this double condition of mine. Moreover, the first death reported was a friend of mine. His name was Torreglosa. His brains were smashed by a bullet, but he died resisting the U.S. invasion. Torreglosa, a Black Panamanian, died with an AK-47 in his hands.

My friend Torreglosa was part of the resistance in Panama, but our babies, our women, our elder folks, they were innocent victims. Again, they were non-white. I will stress this because it is my strong belief that racism was in the center of the brutal invasion of Panama.

Blacks have been part of the oppressed people in our country since very, very early. During the canal construction the U.S. government introduced apartheid in Panama. Yes, Black Panamanians knew about apartheid before South Africans. This was 1907. The U.S. government structured a gold and silver roll system. White laborers were paid in gold currency, non-whites were paid in silver. They both drank from different water fountains, lived in separate barracks, of course with separate and different conditions, separate health services, all the works that still prevail at present in South Africa. The United States called it gold and silver rolls.

These racial practices became part of the social conduct of our government in Panama. Throughout our national history, racism has always been present. Our ruling classes have exercised political power with a heavy accent on racism. They even went as far as prohibiting non-white immigration in our 1941 Constitution.

81

I must tell you that the U.S. government has played a major role in Panamanian domestic policy, at least until 1968. So you must understand that the U.S. government has been part of the negative racial practices against Blacks, Mestizos and Mulattos in Panama. This was reinforced, it is my belief, during the U.S. invasion of Panama. I am quite sure that the U.S. military wouldn't have used a Stealth [fighter] bomber, such a destructive missile beast, in the neighborhoods where the non-Blacks reside.

Don't get me wrong. I'm not justifying the use of the F-117 Stealth bomber anywhere. What I'm saying is that it is clear there had to be racist criteria to kill thousands of people, all non-white people. When you look at formal and informal reports that show not one oligarch casualty, you can't think of anything else but racism. I don't.

Let's look at what's happened since the U.S. invasion took place on December 20. Over 18,000 war refugees are stuffed in concentration camps. If the U.S. media were to exhibit views of these camps, you would see babies, children, women, and elderly folk in those disastrous concentration camps. It has been terrible. And all these babies, all these women, all these men, all these elderly folks, aside from having in common being Panamanian, they also have in common the color of their skin.

The U.S. troops have carried out five major raids in the Republic of Panama, they claim seeking arms and drugs. Do you want to know where those raids were conducted?

The U.S. media won't tell you. I'll tell you. Most of you present here tonight may not know Panama. But these raids were carried out in Curundú, Cerro, Cocowalo, Santa Marta, and San Joaquín. As I said, most of you aren't Panamanian. Those five neighborhoods are inhabited by hundreds of thousands of Blacks, Mestizos and Mulattos. Over 2,000 men and women were put away in barbed-wire improvised jails. This happened just two weeks ago.

Thousands of people have lost their jobs since December 20th. Twelve thousand in the public sector, as Mr. Alemán stated. Mr. Héctor Alemán, Secretary General of the Public Servants Association in Panama, is here tonight. He could tell you who are the folks that have been fired in the last three months. He can tell you which is the color of their skin.

Those are some of the things that are taking place in our newly installed democracy. And do you know who are the folks in power today? Panama is an array of ethnic groups and races. Approximately 60% Mestizos and Mulattos, 20% Black, 10% Indigenous, and 5% white or what we could call white in Panama. Do you know which one of these groups is in power?

Take a look at our President and Vice President. They don't look like any of the members of this delegation. And those of you who have been in Panama, those Panamanians present here tonight, you know as I do that people like us are the majority in Panama.

They claim they have installed democracy in Panama. I challenge them. There is more racism in Panama today. You must be aware of this.

Finally, a special request. Today I was informed at City College that there is a proposal to extend an honorary doctorate to General Colin Powell, chief of the Joint Chiefs of Staff of the U.S. Armed Forces. This is planned to take place in the upcoming graduation ceremony in June at City College. He is Black, somehow. But make us proud of the decent Americans just like you present here tonight. Thank you.

[Editor's note: After the students announced there would be demonstrations against him, General Colin Powell canceled his appearance at City College.]

Cecilio Simón

They Invaded the School
of the Only Black Dean

*Speech by Cecilio Simón, Dean of the
School of Public Administration of the
University of Panama.*

I became the first Black dean of the School of Public Administration. I am not a clerk in the Canal Zone because they wouldn't give me a job, they say I am too radical.

And because I am radical, I was kicked out of my office. A mob went into my office the 5th of March and said, "You're not the dean." The first elected Black dean was kicked out of the university.

And you know why? Because on the 20th of December, at 1:00 o'clock, I was calling to all you who would listen to me and saying it's a shame that a big country like the United States is killing my people.

And that very night, I got in contact with people, not only in the United States, but in the Caribbean. And from that moment, I decided that even if I didn't have a weapon in my hands, I had my tongue and my brains to combat imperialism.

They invaded my school in the university. Ramsey Clark saw the troops sleeping in my office. A sergeant major named Montana was sleeping in my office. They were walking around my office. The only school in the university that was invaded was my school, the Black dean's school.

The only dean they were told to arrest was this Black dean. They arrested me for two and a half hours. But they didn't keep me because when they told me I was wanted for arrest, I went with the vice rector and other deans for them to witness the arrest.

From that moment there was a massive campaign against the people who rejected the invasion and opposed the installation in Panama of the narco-oligarchy.

Why call it that? A guy named Carlos Eleta was jailed in Macon,

Georgia, and after the invasion they freed him. You know why? Because he was the CIA connection to finance the election in Panama. He is right now in Panama as a hero of that narco-oligarchy government.

The president of the Supreme Court was named in the case of a bank that was laundering money [the Dadeland Bank]. The president of the Supreme Court of this narco-oligarchy government! But the President of the so-called government is also a member of that same bank. And the Vice President, the one with the bloody shirt—he was wearing a bloody shirt but that wasn't his blood, that was his Black bodyguard's blood—they say he was one of the owners of the Dadeland Bank. A narco Vice President.

Why so many sophisticated weapons to get what they call a narco-general, in order to install a narco-oligarchy government? I can't understand that. [From audience: "We have a narco-President of the United States!"]

You said it, not me, because probably they'd indict me.

When I go back to Panama, I'm sure that I will be in jeopardy. But I told those who tried to kick me out of the college—tried, they haven't got it yet—that I grew up in Chorrillo, and I know what the *sueco* is. You know what the *sueco* is? Wooden slippers. And I know the *parrilla*. Okay? And I know the slimy yard. I am not afraid of these symbols of poverty because that is my roots.

We want to fight.

[Holds up a paper.] This is a permission to travel issued to a member of our legislature. A member of the legislative corps has to get permission from [U.S. General] Marc Cisneros. Here is his signature, the imperial seal, so we can travel through our streets.

[Reads document.]

"Office of Headquarters, Joint Task Force, Panama, Fort Clayton, Panama. Memorandum for United States Forces in Panama. Subject: Authorization to travel during curfew hours to conduct emergency business/operations.

"1) This letter authorizes the following individual to travel after curfew hours to conduct emergency business/operations in performance of essential duties. Name: H. L. Cadías Castillo. Social Security ID No.: 758151. Organization or agency: Asamblea Legislativa.

"2) All members of U.S. forces should assist the above named individual in his or her performance of essential duties by insuring unrestricted passage from checkpoints, traffic control points, etc. Appropriate reports should be rendered through the chain of command to account for assistance rendered.

"Signed: Marc Cisneros, General, U.S.A., Commander U.S. Army South, Deputy Commander Joint Task Force, Panama."

This memo was signed just last week. And they say they are *civilistas* [supporters of civilian government]. Well, we have a military dictatorship in Panama. In every office, there is a high-ranking official of the U.S. Army and a member of the State Department as controller of the so-called government of Panama.[1]

Do you want to know the name of the controller of the President? His name is General Gann. And you know the name of the controller of the Minister of Education? His name is Captain Vargas. So they get rid of a military dictator that they didn't like and they install *their* military dictatorship.

So friends, comrades, the only way to be free is to know reality and transform facts. That' the only way. And we come here for you to exercise your freedom, because you are not free, you are not receiving correct information. And when you are free, I'll invite you to join me in the struggle to kick out Uncle Sam's army from Panama.

---

1. See Pentagon flowchart on pp. 50-51 listing U.S. personnel assigned as controllers to members of the Endara government.

Additional Reports, Interviews and Documents

Teresa Gutierrez and Valerie Van Isler

Six Months After the Invasion: Growing Crisis and Resistance

Exactly six months after the assault on their country, on June 20, 1990, over 30,000 people demonstrated in Panama City to condemn the U.S. invasion and continuing occupation. Two representatives of the Independent Commission of Inquiry were in Panama at the time on a two-and-a-half-week fact-finding mission to look into the current situation in the country. Teresa Gutierrez, Project Co-Director of the Commission, and Commission member Valerie Van Isler, Executive Director of the Undercurrents Project of WBAI, filed the following report on their findings.

Objective of Trip

One of the main purposes of our trip was to assess the current situation in Panama, particularly developments over the previous three months. The Commission interviewed over 65 people in order to obtain first-hand testimony. Some of the issues the delegation looked at were: political repression, casualties, racism, conditions for children, and the economic and political crisis of the Bush/Endara Administration.

While our delegation tried to focus the interviews on the events of the last three months, we found that most of the people we met had an overwhelming need to talk about December 20, 1989—the night of the invasion. The political activists we spoke to concluded that the people of Panama had not yet had the opportunity to collectively assess and evaluate what really happened on the night of the invasion. Everyone said that the Panamanians had been in shock right after the invasion and were just beginning to come out of it. In addition, for most of the people we spoke to, it was the first time they had had the opportunity to speak to people from the United States who opposed the invasion and were not subtly or overtly hostile to them.

In this context, the June 20 march called by the Committee to Recapture Sovereignty was very significant. It was the first time that a broad spectrum of people and organizations—representing public sector workers, human rights workers, students, political activists, women and refugees—had united in a coalition to publicly show their profound opposition to the invasion and occupation and their growing anger with the Bush/Endara administration.

Repression since the Invasion

The 30,000 people who participated in the march did so in spite of conditions of extreme repression in Panama. According to Graciela Dixon, legal counsel for the war refugees and an organizer for the Committee to Recapture Sovereignty, several march organizers had received threatening phone calls before the demonstration. Several rank and file workers from the state-owned electric company, IRHE, told us they were subtly informed that if seen at the demonstration, they would lose their jobs. Workers from a number of government ministries told us the same thing.

The day before the demonstration, pro-government newspapers ran large front-page headlines with the message, "Noriegistas to march tomorrow," even though the demonstration reflected many points of view, including groups that had been critical of General Noriega.

A thread running through almost all the interviews was that the U.S. occupation had brought a new kind of "psychological terrorism" to Panama. Rafael Olivardía, a leader in the War Refugees Committee, said that the same U.S. military which had bombed the neighborhood of El Chorrillo, killing women and children, is now "housing" the homeless war refugees at Albrook air base. Celia Sanjur, editor of Diálogo Social, an opposition magazine, said that contrary to government propaganda, the United States invaded Panama to show that they were "the owners of the world." Today, she added, U.S. troops are in the police precincts and government ministries, and are involved in all aspects of Panamanian life.

In just about every interview, Panamanians told us that to this day U.S. soldiers interfere in their daily lives, in everything from traffic accidents to marital disputes. On several occasions, we were able to see this for ourselves. While we were conducting street interviews and taking photographs in El Chorrillo, an unmarked patrol car passed by. The car was driven by a Panamanian member of the Fuerzas Públicas. Sitting next to him was a U.S. soldier in uniform.

We also visited one of the many police precincts now being run by U.S. forces and took photos of them inside the building, as well as of their "Hummer" vehicles parked outside.

On July 4, as we left an interview with Olga Mejía, a traffic accident occurred nearby. Two U.S. soldiers soon arrived and took control, giving orders to Panamanians.

Later that same night, a U.S. soldier and two Panamanians came to the door of Ms. Mejía's house at 11:30 p.m., allegedly looking for her husband.

On another occasion, the evening before a scheduled meeting between our delegation and Professor Milsiado Pinzón of the University of Panama in Chitre province, U.S. and Panamanian troops visited his house, also around 11:30 p.m. They said it was in reference to a traffic issue.

Professor Pinzón met with our delegation the next day at the university, which is about three-and-a-half hours from Panama City, and talked to us about the "nation building" plan the United States has for Panama, called "Civic Action." In the Chitre area, U.S. troops are prominently building roads. Professor Pinzón believes this building up of the infrastructure is part of a plan to further militarize Panama and make permanent the U.S. military presence there, which according to the Canal Treaties should end in the year 2000. The professor says that it is widely believed in Chitre that the Endara regime has agreed to a U.S. plan to build a port for nuclear submarines in the area.

René Ríos, an Indigenous man from the Kuna nation, gave us testimony on the presence of U.S. troops on the Panama-Colombia border. Ríos is a resident of San Blas and fought during the invasion. He said one of the first things U.S. troops did after the invasion was ask for drugs—specifically marijuana. He told us that there are now more drugs being sold in the area than before the invasion.

Ríos said that the presence of U.S. troops had increased over the months since the invasion, as evidenced by their occupation of new buildings and the many helicopters flying overhead. He said that U.S. troops now play the role of immigration officials, patrolling the border and asking people for their identification.

In addition to the continued presence of the invading U.S. troops, "psychological terrorism" takes on other forms. The Bush/Endara regime is carrying out a sophisticated, intense campaign to slander and vilify the nationalist sentiments of those who want a free and sovereign Panama. Widespread harassment, threats to people's lives, the loss of jobs, and rumors of imminent arrests are used to discourage any resistance.

Julio Ortega is an example of how this tactic has backfired, for the invasion has deepened his nationalist sentiment. Mr. Ortega was the Director of Channel 2 television in Panama City until December 20. A former U.S. ally, he worked for Voice of America until 1988. As the Reagan-Bush Administration launched its economic sanctions and other aggressions, he began to criticize the United States for violating Panama's sovereignty. A critic of General Noriega, Mr. Ortega feels that any problems with the former government were Panamanian problems and did not justify the invasion and massacre. He has now joined the swelling ranks of the unemployed and discontented.

Over 18,000 people have been fired from their jobs so far. Many members of FENASEP (the union of public service workers), including workers from various government ministries, told us that every day they dreaded getting a "pink slip." People on the job are afraid to talk about the invasion or occupation or criticize the government for fear of being labeled a thug or a criminal.

The Commission was also told that there is a list of some 300 doctors who have been called before a new medical ethics commission set up by the Endara government. Doctors we spoke to said that about 45 physicians have already been questioned and are no longer being allowed to work in the health-care system of Panama. They characterize this as a medical inquisition and part of the climate of political repression.

Effects on Children

The fear of retaliation is so pervasive that even children are afraid to speak up. The Commission interviewed Berta Vargas, a Bolivian who is director of the Emergency Program of the Methodist Church. The program was established specifically to deal with the effects of the invasion. On that night, the church received many requests for help. Since then, because of the dismissals and the general economic crisis, the church has been deluged with three times the usual number of appeals for assistance.

"At any one given time," said Ms. Vargas, "we had more than 100 people asking for food and other help—people fired from San Miguelito, members of FENASEP, workers from the Social Security department, teachers, vendors, people who lost their jobs and positions as a result of the looting. Many more said they were being fired because they had worked with the previous regime. Others were being told that they had vacation time coming and should go on vacation. Under these circumstances, people can't make any mistakes on the job."

She talked about the plight of children. "Through our work we began to discover a large number of orphans. We have attended to 40 families, and of these we have 67 orphans. But these are only the ones we have reached. I think they have big problems. For example, one child came to the office and he didn't want to cry. He was nine years old. I thought maybe he had a problem with machismo and that's why he didn't want to cry. I would tell him he should cry. And he said, 'I can't cry, because if I cry, they'll find out I have a dead father.' Why don't you want to say your father died? I asked him. 'Because my school partners will say that my father was a criminal and belonged to the Dignity Battalions.' After the interview, we found out his father wasn't a member of the Battalions or anything. It was just that someone notified him that El Chorrillo was burning and his mother lived there, so he went out to that area. He hasn't been seen since. This is one case, but there are many children in this situation, without being able to explain or to say what is happening with their parents."

On her work with the children of the Albrook refugee camp, Ms. Vargas told us, "The mothers tell us that the children have nightmares, they are afraid to be by themselves, afraid of whatever noise. When they see people gathering or certain movements, they think the experience of the invasion is going to be repeated."

Mothers of small children and social workers told us that they view the many bomb threats directed against the elementary schools as part of psychological warfare to keep the population intimidated. Eloida, a member of the Journalists Union and mother of two, said her children are frequently forced to evacuate their school buildings and go home because of bomb scares.

The Commission delegation spoke with several doctors who were working in the hospitals during the invasion and at the time of our visit were still treating "war traumas." We asked one of the doctors if children had any special problems six months after the attack. He replied:

"I can say that even now if the children hear a helicopter, they become very nervous. I work with patients in the hospital, and the nurses tell me that the children cannot sleep whenever a helicopter is near. There are teachers in the schools who say that many of the children have real problems, especially in the San Miguelito, Chorrillo and Tocumen neighborhoods, the places most heavily bombed. The people who lived in Chorrillo are now in the Albrook refugee camp—an old U.S. airplane hangar with almost 600 plywood cubicles, each one nine feet long by nine feet wide for each family. At present, about 2,300 displaced Panamanians are living there, most of them very young children and women. There are many, many cases of infections and diarrhea, as well as a very pernicious form of meningitis."

A pediatrician told us that at least four children have died of meningitis. He also has been treating these smallest victims of the invasion. In some cases, he had to use sedatives and other medications to ease the night-mares, anxiety attacks, and screaming fears of these children.

Asked about the medical consequences of the invasion for women, another doctor told us that during the invasion itself, there were many problems with spontaneous abortions, miscarriages, and even women who died on the delivery table. Now, as the occupation continues, there is a reported increase in the number of premature deliveries, which is unusually high. This is undoubtedly connected to the economic problems which have deepened for the many Panamanians who have been fired from their public service jobs by the Endara government and cannot afford the costs of medication and treatment.

Economic Crisis

The official national unemployment rate in Panama is now 35%. However, Héctor Alemán, General Secretary of FENASEP, and Mauro Murrillo, President of CNTP (National Confederation of Panamanian Workers), dispute even that figure as much too low. In Colón, the official rate is 52%.

Gerardo Gonzales of the PRD (Revolutionary Democratic Party), a leader of the opposition in the National Assembly and former Vice President of Panama under General Omar Torrijos, told the Commission that the economic and political crisis in the country is growing. He says the GNP is down by more than 25%. A conservative member of the Assemby has put the loss to Panama from the invasion at $1 billion, a figure Gonzales says is too low.

On July 2, the Panamanian electric company, currently under government control, held a lengthy forum with IRHE workers about privatization. According to an account of this meeting in the major press, the forum was held to discuss the "advantages" of privatizing the electric company. The U.S. Information Service, through a Panamanian AFSCME local, also asked for a private meeting with FENASEP labor leaders on July 3 to discuss privatization.

Growing Resistance

While in Panama, the Commission delegation encountered discontent and resistance indicating a shift away from the Endara government. Two priests, Conrado Sanjún and Joe Cummins, told us that while they had been very critical of some of the policies of General Noriega, the invasion has not brought about what people were led to believe would happen. They are concerned that the Endara government has not taken measures to independently assess the casualties.

They made an appeal to the Ministry of Control to include a question

Demonstration in Panama City on June 20, 1990 demanding U.S. troops go home. Present are refugees from Colón. Photos: Teresa Gutierrez

in the 1990 census on the missing or dead, to help ascertain the extent of the casualties from the invasion, but their request was denied. Other concerns they expressed to us were the lack of funds to help the refugees, and the fact that drugs have become more prevalent in the country. Father Conrado said he thought this was odd, since the Endara government was supposedly installed to end drug trafficking.

In the two-and-a-half weeks the Commission delegation was in Panama, the growing unrest and opposition could be seen in a prison rebellion, a strike by university professors against privatization in Chitre, two student demonstrations, an occupation of the Public Administration department, a hunger strike in Colón, two major demonstrations, and a walkout in the National Assembly. All this points to the inability of the Bush/Endara government to end the crisis and stabilize the country.

The Committee to Recapture Sovereignty concludes that resistance and the unity of the opposition forces are growing. These forces, which joined together for the June 20 demonstration, include the Association of the Families Who Fell or Disappeared on December 20, the War Refugees Committee, the Political Prisoners Committee, the National Committee for the Fired (CONADE), Mothers of the Martyrs, the Revolutionary Workers Party, the Torrijos Tendency (La Tendencia Torrijista), the Peoples Party (Partido del Pueblo), the Social Workers Party, organizations of students from the University of Panama, and several trade unions (FENASEP, CNTP and the Union of Journalists). As is clear from their names, many of these groups have been formed since the invasion to address the many urgent problems it has caused.

Proclamation of the Patriotic Forces

This proclamation was adopted on June 6, 1990, by dozens of Panamanian organizations. The demonstration referred to took place two weeks later on June 20, six months after the invasion, and is described in the previous chapter.

The history of the Panamanian nation constitutes a painful road of struggle against colonization and domination by the brigands and pirates of yesterday and today. For the past five centuries the domination of our land has been arrogantly attempted through the never-ending subjugation of our people.

Our patriots won our independence from Spain and separated us from Colombia so that we would be free and sovereign and in possession of our own destiny.

More recently, the struggle from one generation of Panamanians to the next has had to confront, again and again, the hegemonic interests of the United States, the anti-nationalist forces, the prophets of surrender, lies, deception and false hopes, because these constitute the only obstacle to the realization of the Panamanian Nation.

Today, faced with the most brutal attempt to liquidate Panamanian national consciousness, we the undersigned, in the name of the organizations of the people, of the workers, students, neighborhood groups, organizations of the rural population, of intellectual personalities, professionals and business people, committed to the defense of our sovereignty and national dignity, have joined together this day, June 6, 1990, in order to:

I. *Denounce* before the world the United States Army invasion of our country on December 20, 1989, which violated the sovereign rights and the national self-determination of Panama, producing with this act of colossal barbarism the death of more than 4,000 Panamanians, leaving many more wounded and injured and more than 20,000 without homes, which were bombarded pitilessly, generating material destruction valued at $2 billion nationally, the rounding up of more than 5,000 people into concentration camps (many of whom are still being held without charges of any kind), forcing many patriots into political exile, raising the unemployment rate to over 30% of the population, and finally adding still more to the misery of the Panamanian people who have been the victims of the plundering of our natural resources since 1903 at the hands of U.S. imperialism;

II. *Repudiate* the occupation regime imposed by Washington and upheld exclusively on the points of the bayonets of the invading army so that it may carry out its functions as a puppet government behind a democratic facade to hide its true anti-national, oligarchic and anti-people essence, which voided any representative legitimacy by the treason of providing a cover for the genocide of December 20, revealing in a few short months its zeal to mortgage the entire country in fulfillment of the dictates of the International Monetary Fund, the World Bank and the Agency for International Development, showing its repressive and anti-democratic nature by not hesitating to repress the refugees of El Chorrillo and the urban squatters movement—those living on the edge, occupying vacant lots in improvised dwellings—when they have gone out to demand their rights, by firing more than 15,000 public employees, by beginning the process of privatization of state-owned enterprises, by confirming their true identity as enemy of the workers with the reform of the Labor Code and by practicing the most scandalous nepotism;

III. *Redeem* the memory of the martyrs who fell defending our Fatherland from the invasion and the genocide of December 20, as they, the combatants of the Defense Forces, of the Dignity Battalions, and civilians who rose up in fulfillment of their constitutional obligations, are worthy descendants of the Panamanian national heroes who by their valor and with their blood have been, for generation after generation, forging our national identity, defending our land and our sovereignty from the foreign invader;

IV. *Summon* all of the Panamanian people to accompany the War Refugees of El Chorrillo in the demonstration they will be holding to demand just compensation for their lost homes and possessions this coming June 20, on which date will be commemorated six months since the brutal aggression was perpetrated by the U.S. Army, and similarly, convene the Third National Congress in Defense of Sovereignty and the Right to Live, so that we may deliberate and jointly resolve how we Panamanians will expel the Yankee invaders, achieving our full National Liberation and complete sovereignty over all of the territory of Panama;

V. *Call* on all of the peoples of the world, especially our sisters and brothers in Latin America and the United States, to actively express their repudiation of this occupation and to collaborate by every means necessary to expel the invasionary forces, because the fate of our people, the peoples of this hemisphere, hangs in the balance here; whether in the future the United States carries out further invasions and genocide in our Americas in order to silence the fervent aspirations of our peoples to be free will depend on the victorious resistance in Panama to the Yankee occupation.

The moment has come for us to temper our forces and to demonstrate to the world that on our native Isthmian soil there beat the hearts of patriots prepared to reclaim the traditions of struggle of the molders of our national identity and fulfill the historical mission of forging a Panama that fully enjoys its national sovereignty!

For sovereignty and the right to live!

U.S. occupation army out now!

Human Rights Organizations Must Analyze U.S. Motives

*The following letter is a response by the
Commission for the Defense of Human
Rights in Central America (CODEHUCA) to
a report by Americas Watch on Panama.*

June 5, 1990

Americas Watch
1522 K Street, NW, Suite 910
Washington, DC 20005
Dear Americas Watch:

Re: AW report on "The Laws of War and the Conduct of the Panama
Invasion, May 1990"

   CODEHUCA writes this letter in response to your report on Panama.
We write this letter in the spirit of furthering the work being done in the
aftermath of the United States invasion of Panama. As you may know, we
have referred to the invasion as a massacre, and we are still doing a great
deal of work on this issue.
   As we are in agreement with many parts of the AW report, we will set
out here our differences, in the hopes that AW and other organizations
might continue to investigate the enormity of the destruction of the
invasion, in the final hope of rendering some justice for Panama and
particularly the victims.
   This report will take up issues in the order that they are set out in your
report.
   N.B. The day after you receive this letter, we will be sending it out on
PEACENET. We do this in the hopes of keeping this issue alive in the minds

of the U.S. public—or perhaps it is better to say, in the hopes of awakening the U.S. public to some of what their government does in their name.

At page 2, you state: "The report does not address the matter of the legality or illegality of the decision made by President Bush to invade a foreign country." CODEHUCA (that unequivocally condemns this invasion on legal and moral grounds) thinks that it is not possible to fairly analyze what has happened in Panama, even when assessing the situation only with respect to international humanitarian law, without judging the legality of the invasion.

At page 30 your report states that "it is thus puzzling that the U.S. occupation forces took such an ambivalent attitude toward (the enforcement of the provisions of the III Geneva Convention of 1949 with respect to the treatment of prisoners of war)."

CODEHUCA does not find this "puzzling" at all. We believe that if one were to study the illegality of the invasion one would have to refute the four "justifications" given by President Bush (protect lives of U.S. citizens, defend the Canal treaties, fight against the international trafficking of drugs, and further the fight in favor of democracy) and one would have to question further as to why they did invade.

CODEHUCA is of the opinion that the invasion was far more than a surgical strike, that it was a full-scale invasion to wipe out the entire Panamanian military and security forces. Moreover, that this was done for reasons of strategic U.S. interests in Central America, interests that depend in large part on the huge military infrastructure that exists in Panama.

CODEHUCA thinks it is obvious the United States wants a government in place in Panama that will be more conducive to retaining the U.S. military presence after the year 2000 (date when, according to the Torrijos-Carter Treaties, the United States is to have dismantled and withdrawn all of its military presence).

The importance of asking the question why the United States invaded is not to delve into idle political speculation. The importance is that the United States takes military/political decisions based on self-interest to intervene directly or indirectly in Central American affairs. The result of these militaristic and interventionist decisions has everything to do with the violation of human rights and great human suffering in Central America.

CODEHUCA sees that it is imperative that human rights organizations analyze U.S. motives from the perspective of the three generations of human rights (that includes the right to sovereignty, the right to self-determination, and the right to peace) and from the perspective of the hundreds of thousands of victims.

Thus, the lack of respect for the Geneva rules on the treatment of prisoners is not puzzling—it has everything to do with U.S. plans to dismantle the nationalistic Panamanian defense and security forces and crack down on political opposition (see report of first CODEHUCA delegation to Panama); and these U.S. plans have everything to do with the resultant massacre, and the crisis in which Panamanians are now living.

At p. 4, the AW report states: "Unfortunately, the debate over the Panama invasion has been narrowed to the number of civilian casualties." In one sense this is true. However, CODEHUCA feels that it is important to continue focusing a lot of attention on the actual numbers for two reasons.

Firstly, in the realm of international politics CODEHUCA is of the opinion that the United States, supported by complicit media coverage, has already legitimized the invasion. As far as international opinion and the international media is concerned, it was okay to invade and kill (using U.S. figures) 500-600 civilians and soldiers.

Thus, as unsavory as it is, CODEHUCA is trying to show that it was far worse than what we are being told. As unsavory as it is, CODEHUCA feels that the U.S. conscience will be affected only if shown that this was a massacre. Secondly, on humanitarian and moral grounds, only with a full inquiry will the families of the disappeared have a chance to find the bodies of their loved ones and give them a decent burial.

The AW report states, at p. 4: "nor are we (Americas Watch) persuaded that there has been a deliberate attempt to hide the real numbers." CODEHUCA believes the contrary is true. Both reports address this issue, amongst other issues.

With respect to the actual number of persons killed, it is this very process of investigation that the United States is trying to prevent, because the true extent of the numbers killed (CODEHUCA is of the opinion that the real numbers are closer to 2,000, if not more) would show the world the real picture of the U.S. defensive surgical strike, called Just Cause.

CODEHUCA invites AW and other organizations to read our second delegation report to Panama. Its main focus was to look at the numbers of killed persons. The reader will see that many obstacles—some intentional and some due to confusion—exist, preventing a real determination. The reader will also see that much circumstantial evidence exists (evidence that should be investigated more deeply) suggesting strongly that the numbers are much higher than the 300-600 normally quoted.

Thirdly, the numbers of killed should be honestly and openly investigated for legal reasons—the invasion was illegal, and the U.S. government owes indemnification to Panama, for the material destruction, and to the family members of the persons the United States killed.

While the recently approved loans by the U.S. government of some $400,000,000 may help regenerate the Panamanian economy that the United States almost single-handedly destroyed, it is of the utmost cynicism that they help destroy an economy, make the victim dependent on them for recovery, and then turn around and "loan" them money, putting them further into debt with the very country that destroyed their economy.

For humanitarian reasons and for the reasons of legal indemnification, it is of the utmost importance that a full investigation be undertaken to determine the number of persons killed by the U.S. military.

At p. 8, the report states that: "If someone alleges for example that 4,000 died, whereas a more accurate estimate is only 10% of that, then the media unfortunately but naturally takes it that the lower figure is 'acceptable.'"

Based on what happened in the invasion of Panama, CODEHUCA disagrees with this comment. It is not always true that the media naturally takes the lower figure. Depending on the nature of U.S. interests, it is quite clear that the media has and will present inflated figures if it is in the interests of U.S. policy. In this case, it is in U.S. interest to minimize the image of the damage and death caused.

CODEHUCA deals with this point concerning the media, not to indulge in media bashing, but rather to point out that due to the soft image created in part by the media, the invasion has been generally accepted as a legitimate U.S. action. It is this very acceptance that presents a huge obstacle to persons and organizations trying to get legal indemnification for the persons killed, and trying to get a decent burial for the disappeared. Only international pressure will "move" or pressure the U.S. government to reassess its illegal invasion, and pay proper compensation.

The pacifying role of the media, and the use of very low estimates of killed persons, figures that echo official U.S. figures, serves to put a blanket of silence over, and an image of democracy around a very battered and worn-down country.

At p. 9, the AW report states: "Bodies were buried in common graves, but records were kept to allow exhumations when relatives came forward with further information."

The second CODEHUCA report deals at length with the obstacles facing family members who are seeking the disappeared. Moreover, direct testimony and the first exhumation of a common grave (that of the Jardín de Paz, exhumed in April), show conclusively that records were not kept for all persons buried in the common graves.

For CODEHUCA, this is one case of circumstantial evidence that exists that goes to undermining the low figures presented by the U.S. government, and echoed in the AW report.

Moreover, as set out in the first CODEHUCA report, we received direct testimony from a man who had had to flee Chorrillo who saw U.S. soldiers incinerating bodies on the spot and burying them in small holes they had dug there. We do not have an indication of how many bodies were dealt with in this way, but again it is evidence that the numbers of killed are much higher.

At p. 9: "There have been references to the deliberate burning of bodies. We were not able to obtain confirmation of this fact. [See paragraph above for CODEHUCA'S response.] We believe that it could not have involved more than a few bodies; in addition, the procedure would not have resulted in the complete destruction of all traces of the remains. ..."

CODEHUCA agrees that the incineration procedure could not result in the complete destruction of all traces. It is for this reason that CODEHUCA believes there is a concerted cover-up effort discouraging and preventing people and groups from carrying out proper investigations.

One Panamanian group, la Asociación de Caídos del 20 de Diciembre (see Second CODEHUCA Report), alleges that there are at least 12 common graves in Panama. To date, they have succeeded in having only one common grave (Jardín de Paz) exhumed.

The Asociación plans to continue with their efforts until all the reported disappeared persons have been located. The official body (grupo de enlace) set up to receive denunciations concerning disappeared persons has received some 1,400 cases so far (up until the end of March) and the Asociación has received some 1,500 (see Second Report).

At p. 11, the AW report states: "Most (bodies) were counted once they were in a morgue or in a hospital." We received testimony stating that many bodies never went to a morgue or hospital—rather they were buried on the spot, or taken directly, in body bags, to common graves. Again, CODEHUCA does not have and, because the U.S. Southern Command controls most if not all of the pertinent information (see First and Second Reports concerning the setting up of a "shadow U.S. government" that is exercising a fair degree of administrative control over the vital sectors of the state, and this includes the hospitals), could not obtain exact figures. But, again, this is evidence of many more deaths than accounted for.

At p. 13, the AW report states that "the method for counting the number of Panamanian soldiers killed by U.S. soldiers has an obvious, built-in bias on the side of overcounting." While this may be true in the case of a conventional confrontation—soldier-to-soldier combat—in the case of the U.S. invasion, the U.S. military relied primarily on its air forces, and a high degree of bombarding of civilian and military targets, thus eliminating the possibility of counting at all the number of victims.

CODEHUCA would argue that given the type of invasion—over-kill is a word that many persons and organizations have used—the built-in bias would be towards the low side.

At p. 17, in a footnote, the AW report states that: "We heard unverifiable rumors that other Chorrillo neighbors claimed to have seen U.S. troops deliberately setting fires to the houses."

CODEHUCA received testimony from people that saw U.S. troops entering the houses of Chorrillo, flushing the persons living there out into the street without a chance to gather their belongings, and then deliberately setting fire to the homes. This is covered in our First Report. We can make this testimony available to AW, or to any group that asks for it.

At pp. 17-18, the AW report states: "It is evident that the buildings adjacent to the Panamanian command forces could have been the legitimate object of attack or defense, and consequently could have been hit by either side."

At p. 20, the AW report states: "The attack on the Comandancia was the single episode ... that generated the highest number of civilian dead and wounded, ... It was not however a case of indiscriminate fire, nor of fire purposefully directed at civilians, since it is clear that the target was the Comandancia." For CODEHUCA, this is not so clear at all.

In our First Report, CODEHUCA gives testimony from residents of some 15-story apartment buildings referred to that are very close to the Comandancia. Their testimony recounts how their civilian buildings were directly attacked first by air and then ground troops, using high-powered bullets and rocket projectiles. Forty meters away from their building there is an uninhabited white building of some six stories that was under construction at the time of the invasion. *This building does not have one bullet or projectile mark on it.* It suffered no damage.

Thirty meters further away there is another civilian building that was, and still is inhabited, and it suffered direct attack by air and ground troops as well.

CODEHUCA has ample photo coverage of these apartment buildings, clearly showing that the uninhabited one in the middle was left totally alone. CODEHUCA believes this to be strong evidence that the U.S. troops knew they were directly attacking civilian targets.

Moreover, as the AW report mentions, there is the question of proportionality. This question should be looked at more carefully by any group investigating the invasion. CODEHUCA's opinion is that, questions of legitimacy of the invasion aside, it was a clear case of military over-kill against a sleeping population and a totally overwhelmed and overpowered Panamanian army.

At p. 41, the AW report states that "they (the new government) began as democratically elected leaders." Based on the conversations that CODEHUCA had in Panama, no one really questioned that the elections of 1989 were fraudulent, and that the opposition would have won. What CODEHUCA objects to here is the notion that the new government "began" their government (December 20, 1989) as "democratically elected leaders." This is clearly not the case. It is well known they were sworn into power on a U.S. military base, hours after the invasion/massacre had begun. CODEHUCA feels that in no way whatsoever should AW or any organization indirectly legitimize the U.S. invasion, suggesting that the invasion properly imposed democratically elected leaders.

CONCLUSION

This is not an exhaustive criticism of the AW report, nor a full analysis of the invasion. CODEHUCA hopes that AW and other organizations can reflect on our opinions and perhaps send to us their response, or reconsider certain aspects of the report. CODEHUCA is most willing to provide AW and other organizations with information to substantiate our comments.

For the general reader, CODEHUCA encourages you to read the AW report and CODEHUCA reports, and any other information concerning the invasion.

Whatever one's opinions on the number of dead, this issue must be dealt with. The two delegations that CODEHUCA sent to Panama (in January and March) were witness to perhaps the greatest social, economical, political and cultural crisis that Panama has ever lived.

They were witness to a great deal of suffering due, for the most part, to the recent years of economic aggression, culminating in the invasion/massacre of December 20, 1989.

For more information, or to send comments or criticisms, please contact our offices: CODEHUCA, AP 189, Paseo Estudiantes, San José, Costa Rica, Tel - 24 59 70, Fax - 34 29 35; Attention: Grahame Russell.

Euclides Fuentes Arroyo, Union Leader

Human Rights Do Not Exist Here

This is an interview with Euclides Fuentes Arroyo, President of the Journalists Union of Panama and an officer of the Latin American Federation of Journalists. The interview was conducted on March 6, 1990, in Panama City, by a member of the Independent Commission of Inquiry, and was translated from the Spanish by the Commission.

Q. Has there been any change in the freedom of the press from the time of the previous government to the present government?

A. Yes, the newspapers that were closed have been reopened. This means that, on the one hand, there is another source of jobs and one where the people can exercise their freedom of expression. This is favorable in one sense. But in practice, what is actually happening is that there is a limitation to the freedom of expression. This is because the workers in Panama do not find in the newspapers that are being published at this time any of their own concerns being expressed or addressed.

There is genuine freedom of expression for the media owners—for that reason the Inter-American Press Association, which is the organization of newspaper owners, has issued a statement asserting that in Panama, and now in Nicaragua, there has been an improvement in the freedom of expression. But we who are professional journalists, we who live the experience here, can affirm categorically that we, the journalists and members of the Journalists Union and the Typographers Union in Panama specifically, are now victims of a situation in which our members are demanding a recognition of their rights and do not find in these newspapers freedom of speech because these newspapers attack us.

You can look, for example, at today's edition of the newspaper Panamá América. They attack their workers who are calling for recognition of their

107

rights. But they do not publish even a single line, either as news or in the form of press releases, from the unions. So what kind of freedom of speech are we talking about?

This violates a fundamental human right.

Q. Has the ownership of some of the newspapers changed hands since the invasion?

A. There were some newspapers belonging to the Editora Renovación that the opposition newspapers accused of being pro-government. Well, these newspapers no longer exist. These newspapers of the Editora Renovación were taken over *de facto* by the former owners of Panamá América without any legal basis whatsoever, exclusively on the authority of the U.S. tanks.

And when they arrived they took over the installations that belonged to the Editora Renovación, without even a figleaf of legality, without any order from any court. They know very well that they could do precisely what the former owner or the government did when they paid off the debt that was owed to the Banco Nacional, the Social Security bank, and to other banks and creditors of the former owners of Panamá América. This debt was paid off by a consortium in which the government and others participated and they obtained a legal decision, a court order transferring ownership. This group made absolutely no attempt to obtain legal ownership, they simply took advantage of the invasion, obtained the support of the U.S. Army tanks, seized the installations de facto and fired the workers.

Now, they are refusing to pay the workers whom they fired the money they had already earned. This is a clear violation of Panamanian law under the Labor Code.

Q. Is there any evidence of a direct participation of the new government in the formulation of the news?

A. I wouldn't be able to say categorically that there is direct influence in that regard. But it is well known that all the morning newspapers, every morning run the same stories from the government, with the identical orientation. And it's hard to refer to them as news stories, rather they are a product of the same political propaganda. And this is propaganda about the workings of the government. In this sense nothing has changed at all. It has only been a change of faces but the attitude of the former government and the present one in relation to the media is the same. You only get one side of the story. For example, on the question of government layoffs the government says, "There are no massive layoffs." Yet every day there are thousands of government employees thrown out on the streets. And then when the workers protest, this does not appear in the newspapers. Nothing more is heard of this from the government.

And the government uses the same tactic. The government says that it is firing people for political reasons because the workers who are being fired, according to them, belonged to the Dignity Battalions or the CODEPADIs.[1] Lie. They are firing them because this is what is being demanded of the new government by the International Monetary Fund on the one hand, and by members of the same parties as those in the government who want to get their own people into these jobs. They fire the ones who are working there and replace them with their own people. Thus they lie to the public saying, "We are firing so-and-so because he belonged to the Dignity Battalions." The Dignity Battalions were formed to defend the nation's sovereignty. And so whether they were members or not, they are fired.

The IMF and the World Bank demand that in order to pay the foreign debt, they must cut government expenditures. Then on the other hand, they promised their political supporters jobs and now they are demanding that these promises be fulfilled. And for them the easiest ones to fire are the public employees.

Q. Has there been any interference in the functioning of the press by the U.S. officials since the invasion?

A. On Friday an item appeared in various newspapers in which the names appear of North American officials who are working in the Panamanian government everywhere from the Ministry of the Presidency to the autonomous government agencies. The U.S. officials are giving the orders.

Q. We have been told of the existence of a list of journalists who have been fired and, because they are on this list, are unable to find work as journalists. What can you tell us about such a list?

A. That is a list that was made as a denunciation. It is a list of journalists who were denounced because we have always held a nationalist position, in defense of the nation's sovereignty, of the nation's dignity. We condemned the invasion because we respect the principle of the right of peoples to self-determination and non-intervention. So, they have accused some 32 of us, before the circuit court, of supposedly having committed a crime. That is, they consider that we have committed a crime for having condemned the U.S. invasion, for having defended the sovereignty and the integrity of our country. To them, this is a crime.

Also they have accused us of rebelling against the duly constituted

---

1. CODEPADIs: Committees in Defense of the Country and Dignity. Unarmed, pro-government, community-based organizations.

authorities. How could we rebel against the duly constituted authorities, on December 20, for example, the day the invasion occurred, if the transmitters were closed during all of those days? On the 20th, the transmitters were only able to function until about noon, because Radio Nacional was bombed. I was unable to leave my house. I was in my house and I couldn't leave because there was no way, they were bombing the whole area, Chorrillo, everywhere you turned, it was dangerous to leave your house. I didn't have a telephone. My telephone was out.

The Constitution of Panama says that in the event of an invasion by a foreign power, Panamanian citizens are obligated to take up arms and defend their country. These gentlemen are so stupid that they have made this accusation against us despite the fact that we are Constitutionally obligated to take up arms. I didn't take up arms quite simply because I didn't have any arms and I couldn't go out, but if that hadn't been the case, we were obligated to do so.

There is a charge pending against 38 of us. Among the accused is Joaquín Belaño, who died 12 years ago. It is completely absurd. It's a matter of repression for repression's sake. So, what rights do journalists have?

We have filed a formal complaint on behalf of the Journalists Union of Panama. There is a list at all the airports and border crossings that those on the list may not leave the country. You may not leave the country because you have been accused. Thus one finds oneself a virtual prisoner in one's own territory.

In my particular case, for example, I am the General Secretary of the Journalists Union of Panama. During the current month, I am the Coordinator of the National Council of Organized Workers, CONATO. I am a trade union leader and in addition I was elected as a director of the Latin American Federation of Journalists [FELAP] at the congress in Acapulco, Mexico, in 1988. If FELAP calls me to attend a meeting, I will be unable to leave the country because my name is on a blacklist. Can you imagine, as a journalist I am unable to leave the country because there is a false accusation against me!

I appeal to any of the human rights commissions, and the amnesty groups wherever they might be, the solidarity groups of all countries, to come to our aid, and tell the government to put an end to this list and to grant Panamanian journalists the right to travel freely within the country and outside of the country. Because now as long as this list exists, there are many journalists like myself who are unable to leave the country or to carry out whatever responsibilities they may have in international organizations.

Our union offices were occupied by the U.S. Army during the first week of the invasion. They installed a barricade and a gun emplacement surrounded by sandbags, as if the children from the Children's Hospital were about to attack them. Our neighbors over here are the sick children from the Children's Hospital. So they set up their machine-guns on our third-floor balcony and their tanks in the courtyard and occupied the building. They holed up here for two weeks before we could get back into our offices. The first union meeting that we were able to hold wasn't until the 18th of January.

Q. How many of your members have lost their jobs?

A. More than 150.

I think it's important to mention that they are reporting here that a number of troops had been withdrawn. This announcement was made just before the anti-drug summit in Cartagena. It appears to me that it was more of a political announcement than anything else, because here in Panama, there are U.S. troops everywhere. They're not merely stationed on the bases. Now with all of the talk about dangerous conditions, and that they dismantled the police force, they are not staying on their bases but they are all over the place. In every part of the country they are going around in their armored cars and their tanks, with their automatic weapons and who knows what.

There is a curfew! A curfew that has lasted for months, since December. The people like to go out and have a good time, visit a friend, have a drink, go dancing—at night, the heat makes one want to get out and get some fresh air—but we can't go out, here we are unable to do anything.

The people who work the night shift are losing their right to a job, the right to live. We are living in a situation as if under the Pinochet regime. This under the guise of a representative democracy.

We are already into the month of March and there is still a curfew. Yesterday there was an announcement by Arias Calderón that the curfew is going to continue. What kind of democracy are we talking about? What kind of demilitarization? We are now more militarized than when Noriega was here. When there was a curfew after the attempted coup of October 3rd [1989], the curfew kept getting shorter and it didn't even last a month. Now we're into the third month of curfew.

We are in a situation where human rights here do not exist. Here, any political figure can be accused of a common crime and they are taken right off to prison.

We Offer Our Lives in the Name of Liberty

The following is a letter written by a member of the Dignity Battalions of Panama who was later killed in combat. His name is withheld at the request of his family. The letter is translated from the Spanish by the Independent Commission of Inquiry.

Dear Sweetheart,

To describe what I have seen breaks one's heart and makes me cry with the pain and fury of all that has happened.

I believe I have started this letter badly but the pain I feel is so great that I couldn't avoid it. Those of my people who are left continue harassing the gringos. The possibilities of their surrendering are very small because their convictions are firm and they cannot accept that the gringos kill our people and that they go through the streets of our country as if loved.

The fighting is a case of "overkill"—we are horribly overwhelmed by the power of their weaponry. When we would attack, and then pull back, the United States would immediately come with their helicopters and bombard—with rockets and bullets—the entire area, without caring about the civilian inhabitants. They had no courage to directly attack the Battalions. They have used incredible amounts of weaponry of new and high technology.

In the night time, they searched for us everywhere from their helicopters with infra-red spotlights.

Where they think we might be hiding, they fire off a rocket with some chemical material.

Given that we have shot down some of their helicopters, now they are bombarding us with the very quick A-37 fighter planes. These planes are

112

far *less* accurate with their bombs—but this isn't their problem—if a bomb falls in a house, it doesn't matter.

Hardly had they finished destroying and leveling the neighborhood of El Chorrillo than they went over to Panamá Viejo, Cerro Batea, San Miguelito, Los Andes, 9 de Enero, San Francisco and I imagine that these are not all.

On two occasions we were coming out of houses where we had gone to eat and rest when the helicopters arrived—two "Cobras"—and blew up both houses.

Now that there are cracks in Eastern Europe, this has given the United States the chance to show itself as the world's police. The balance that existed before between the superpowers is gone and this is dangerous. This we have to tell the Nicas [Nicaraguans], because this show of force was not only against Panama. They might well be preparing their army and the U.S. public for an invasion of Nicaragua, after the elections, to do away with Sandinismo.

I don't know if our car still exists. This you'll have to verify with [name withheld]. Darling, I hope we have not lost the car, but it saved my life. I had to leave in a big hurry. I didn't go to Amador—rather I went to the Balboa Police. All cars that tried to enter Amador were blown up by U.S. tanks.

[Name withheld] saved himself because he changed vehicles, but they destroyed an entire bus full of his troops. First the bus was blasted with rockets and then U.S. troops machine-gunned those still alive. This we found out because one person—wounded—survived to tell us. He escaped and swam across the bay. We visited him in the Santo Tomás hospital.

Another jeep that was entering Amador with seven or eight members of the Dignity Battalions was wiped out by an air attack—total massacre.

On National Avenue, helicopters opened fire on us, even as many people, civilians, were in the streets.

This has been a massacre. I don't have the words to describe it. They killed two of my friends. They were with me and I could not get them out of there. I looked for an ambulance that was going by. When the ambulance went to get them, the U.S. troops opened fire on it.

They are savages. They have a sick fury. They have massacred our people like animals.

In their tanks they have run over the bodies of Panamanians without caring whether they were dead or wounded. They are the same as or worse than the Germans of Hitler.

I am very disappointed with the Panama Defense Forces. They demonstrated that they had neither the preparation nor the disposition nor the conviction to defend our country from the gringo attack.

It is evident to me that the Dignity Battalions have all the necessary patriotic attributes to offer their lives in the name of liberty and against the forces of injustice.

I never underestimated the value of my people, but I can honestly assure you, without any remorse, that I never thought that when the time came to fight for the country, they would be so brave—brave as the liberation fighters that one reads about from the other parts of the world.

History must preserve this.

The Students Were Machine-gunned Before They Could Surrender

This interview with a civilian worker at the Río Hato military base of the Panama Defense Forces was conducted in Panama City on February 23, 1990, by a member of the Independent Commission. The name of the worker is withheld because of fear of reprisals. The interview is translated from the Spanish.

Q. You were at the military base at Río Hato?

A. Yes, I was at the base at Río Hato. I am a civilian—I was engaged in maintenance work at the base.

Located at that base at Río Hato were the Sixth Expeditionary Company, a tank unit of the Machos de Monte, and two schools. One is the officers' school "Benjamín Ruiz." The other is a secondary school [high school] where they have the option of going on to pursue a military career or going on to the university. These students are known as the Tomasitos.

That night of the 19th to the 20th of December we went to bed, but rumors were circulating that the 82nd Division had left the United States and that there was the possibility of an invasion.

Q. What time was this?

A. At about 7 p.m., maybe a little bit later. I think that none of us really believed that an invasion would actually happen, when you took into consideration the overwhelming difference in power between the two countries. I don't think that it would justify an invasion to remove Noriega, if that was its objective. Noriega had been near the base over the weekend taking in the fresh air with a small escort. If they had wanted to capture him they could have done it easily at that time or they could have done it the previous Sunday when he was there near the base in a public place with a friend of his. If there had to be bloodshed, they could have got him at that time with maybe 20 dead or, exaggerating the situation, 30 killed at the maximum—not the thousands of deaths which actually took place. An invasion was not justified to capture Noriega. We never believed this justification.

Then at about a quarter to one in the morning, we heard explosions and the helicopters buzzing the buildings. Then the machine guns started and we ran out of the barracks where we were staying. As there was a full moon, we could clearly see the paratroopers coming down. There was a plan for evacuation of the students, but the barracks were not close together, so the evacuation plan could only be carried out for a small group of students. Another group of students was captured by the U.S. soldiers. There were a number of these students killed.

This was because the U.S. troops didn't realize that they were practically children. They were all under 18 years old. They were machine-gunned before they could surrender. They were unarmed and before they told them to surrender they had opened fire.

Q. Did any of them have any weapons?

A. Among these kids? No, none of them. Some of them went to the armory to try to get weapons but they were not given to them. These were not streetwise kids. Well, anyway, they weren't given any weapons.

Q. How many were killed when they opened fire?

A. I didn't see it myself, but I heard the boys say that there were about 30 killed.

Q. Where were you at this time?

A. I ran towards the mountains, but I stayed close to the base. The helicopters fired at me. At that time I met up with two soldiers who were armed, and four boys, four Tomasitos who were unarmed. The boys were very frightened, they had no idea what the flares were. It was obvious that they had absolutely no military preparation. They have tried to say that this was a military training school but that isn't true.

They used lasers, they used these very large helicopters that fired missiles that caused multiple explosions, powerful explosions. They fired at us with machine guns. There were other bombs, which were very strange. They were strange in the sense that the explosion first produced a white light which then turned red. I have been told that this was the kind of bomb they used here in the neighborhood of El Chorrillo, to burn down the neighborhood. They were different, even the soldiers there had never seen that kind of explosion before.

When I was finally captured, they made me kneel against a wall, they put an M-16 against my neck and they threatened to kill me. The one who did this was very nervous. All of the U.S. soldiers that I saw at that moment seemed very nervous. They were also very young, about 20 years old, and it must have been their first experience in a genuine combat situation and maybe they expected more organized resistance. They seemed very frightened and very nervous.

One of them told the other not to kill me, that they would interrogate me. From there they transferred me to a place where they had the other prisoners. There they had a lot of the boys, the Tomasitos. They held them there tied up, with their hands tied behind their backs with a plastic band. They were treating them very badly there. They hit them, they beat them. There were some wounded and they kept them out in the sun. They were not given any medical attention. They poked them, took their personal belongings away from them like watches and money. They gave the impression that an army of mercenaries had arrived instead of a professional army. There was a scene where one U.S. soldier showed a watch to another and asked him if he liked it. The other one said, "If it works it's mine." And he kept it.

They were also gathering up a fair number of civilian prisoners. The civilians were not treated as badly as the military prisoners. They gathered up, for example, family members, small children, three-year-olds. This little girl was crying and saying that she wanted to go home but they couldn't, the whole family was being held prisoner.

We spent the whole day there, the 20th. They photographed us, took our names.

In the morning they began to look at some of the wounded. There was among them a youth who seemed to be pretty badly wounded—he had been wounded in the abdomen and in both arms. I don't know if they were bullet wounds or from shell fragments or shrapnel but he seemed to be in pretty bad shape. He was stretched out on the floor. Then a U.S. soldier came up, I think he was an officer, and he ordered that he be given medical care.

Q. What time was this?

A. I'm not sure, I think it must have been around 11 o'clock. He was wounded around 1:30 in the morning so he hadn't received any medical attention for about 10 hours. But he was in very bad shape. He was left on the floor, and the floor was really filthy because it was the floor of the auto-mechanics' garage for the base. That's where we were being held.

I was also able to see the inside of one of the barracks, because I asked permission to go to the bathroom. The inside of the barracks was completely incinerated, but it was burned by a different kind of fire; when you touched something it turned to dust, things would seem to be whole, but when you touched them, they would completely disintegrate.

Officially they say there were 23 U.S. soldiers killed. Later I found out that at the Río Hato base two helicopters had been shot down. Already we can add up perhaps 19 dead, which would mean that in the rest of Panama, there would be only four [Americans] killed. That's unbelievable, isn't it? The United States had many more deaths than have been officially acknowledged.

I think that, due to the intensity of the bombardment that was carried out, there had to have been many Panamanian deaths at that base. Because that's where the Machos de Monte were based, the elite troops who had defended Noriega during the attempted coup on October 3rd. There were even reports that that was where they had used a plane that had never been tested in action before, and from which they dropped the first bombs against us. They were experimenting on us.

I was captured at about 5 or 6 a.m. on the 20th and we weren't given anything to eat until noon on the 21st. In the meantime they only gave us water, but in very small quantities. They gave food to the children and the civilian women that they rounded up.

They rounded up the entire civilian population. There are two towns very close to the base. They went to these towns and rounded up all of the males 14 years old and older without any consideration—they arrested old men who, because of their advanced age and physical condition, it was impossible to imagine that they even had the strength to pick up a weapon. They took them prisoner, they took everyone prisoner.

When they were getting ready to transfer us to another location, they were bringing in military prisoners, treating them very badly. For example, one who had been wounded in the leg, they beat him on his wound. One of them said, "This motherfucker is wounded," and they hit him and threw him down on the ground like a sack of potatoes.

On the 21st, after holding us there all morning under the sun, they took us in the planes that carry the paratroopers in to Howard Air Base and from there we were taken to a concentration camp that was set up at an artillery practice firing range, the New Empire range, near the Canal. They were bringing in Panamanian soldiers who they were finding and who were wearing civilian clothes. And from there they transferred us to Balboa High School where they had the refugees who used to live in the neighborhood of El Chorrillo that was right next to the Central Barracks and was burned to the ground and also those who had been prisoners in the Model Jail.

Now, they have placed people on my job to control the rest of the workers. They observe us continually, take note of what we do and what we don't do. This is not to monitor our productivity on the job, but to monitor us politically. We are all subject to being fired at any moment.

Since I was old enough to be aware of my environment, Panama has been a country that was relatively better off than the other Latin American countries that I know about. But during the last two years, with the economic pressure, the poverty level has risen terribly. Before you never saw children begging on the streets, emotionally deranged people going around. The level of alcohol consumption has gone up.

We in Panama are not accustomed to those things and we saw many applauding the fall of Noriega, believing in the promises that substantial economic aid would be forthcoming from the United States. And instead what we are seeing now is the application of the policies of the International Monetary Fund. One of these is the reduction of employment in the public sector, the payment of the foreign debt. This is going to wake up a lot of Panamanians from this illusion they had. I think they are waking up already.

Panama Is a Focus of U.S. Geopolitical Strategy

On April 2, 1990, while appearing in U.S. Federal District Court in Miami for a pretrial hearing, General Manuel Antonio Noriega submitted the following comments on the invasion in writing to two members of the Independent Commission of Inquiry on the U.S. Invasion of Panama, Gavrielle Gemma and Teresa Gutierrez. The translation from the Spanish is by the Independent Commission.

Facing an internal problem of political administration, the National Assembly, popularly elected in 1984 and within its legal authority, replaced President Barletta and named Mr. Del Valle president.

The government of the United States then imposed economic sanctions on Panama, freezing its financial assets in the Banco Nacional in New York and all of the financial assets of the *Panamanian nation*: that is to say, the property of all the people. In addition, it seized goods and seven aircraft of the state enterprise Air Panama, and gradually imposed restrictions on U.S. multinationals, ordering them not to pay taxes to the Republic of Panama, including the medical insurance of many poorly paid workers such as the employees of the Chiriquí Land Co., ESSO, Petro Terminal, Omaha, etc. Above all, the nonpayment of the Canal Annuities was in flagrant violation of international treaties.

The consequences of these arbitrary, illegal, inhuman and colonialist measures were deeply felt and still affect the economy and the life of the Republic of Panama, which is a poor country, in the following areas:

a) Public health: The hospitals, medical supplies, and medical attention to the sick, above all to the children, were compromised and still feel the impact of the inhuman North American actions.

b) Education: The planned curriculum was interrupted and the struggle against illiteracy was suspended, prejudicing the interests of the majority of the population, the poor, those who are unable to send their children abroad to study.

c) Public works: The plan to bring the rural areas into the modern world was halted. The work on rural roads in remote areas of the country affecting the most marginalized population living in improvised housing in the cities broke down, as it did for the indigenous people of the mountains and the jungle areas.

d) The fiscal health of the government and its resources diminished and unemployment increased.

That is to say, every aspect of the country was affected. Economic experts calculate that the national treasury suffered losses of over $2 billion.

The reasons for the invasion of the Republic of Panama by the government of the United States include:

I. The Panamanian isthmus is of strategic importance to the United States! For that reason we see the interest in, and the phobia against Panama rather than Peru or Paraguay or Argentina or Venezuela or Guatemala; because none of them are either the passageway or the focus of geopolitical strategy, they don't have an interoceanic canal, and they are not the geographical center of intercontinental routes.

II. Because of the military bases, the United States has an interest in continuing to maintain troops at the crossroads of the American continent that can be deployed to control South, North and Central America and the Caribbean. The only ideal country in all of the Americas is Panama, with the Atlantic and Pacific regions correlated with the transit distances for air and maritime traffic. In addition, the vegetation and ecology of Panama provide a proving ground with terrain equivalent to that of Colombia and Venezuela and the jungles of Peru and Brazil.

III. The treaties signed by President Carter and Torrijos were to put an end to the armed presence and the military control of a Southern Command in the year 1999. The new United States administration and its "establishment" now consider that it was an error to have signed these treaties and are looking for a way to invalidate them. And for this reason they violate and continue violating their clauses.

IV. The administrator of the Canal is now supposed to be a Panamanian, reversing the majority from North Americans to Panamanians. It was necessary that this should be someone dependable and manageable for the North American government officials in order to continue using their

CIA with its economic resources as the source for other hidden and secret funding not reported to the U.S. Treasury, for covert actions and illegal aggression such as the Iran-Gate operations against Nicaragua.

The consequences of the invasion include:

I. The physical destruction of the country by aerial bombardment and the devastation and destruction of buildings, material goods, etc.

II. Civilian and military deaths, including North Americans, whose death toll has been kept secret and the information denied to the North American people. There are families still searching for their missing relatives who disappeared into common graves or whose bodies were incinerated by flamethrowers. The death and destruction caused by this invasion are kept at reasonable levels and scientifically controlled. Like the devastation at Hiroshima and Nagasaki, one must look at the video-tapes taken during that night to be able to appreciate the magnitude of savagery and *inhumanity.*

III. To install a submissive government that would be committed to granting military and occupational concessions to the United States and to becoming an unconditional ally against other Latin American nations. This submissive government will go so far as supporting the destruction of the Carter-Torrijos Treaties and the ceding of military bases for expansion and technological control and installations such as Isla Galeta to be used as a listening post to eavesdrop from Panama on other countries in the region.

The United States since the signing has been gradually and increasingly violating the Carter-Torrijos Treaties, becoming more brazen in its violations since 1985 and showing less and less restraint, especially in the years 1987, 1988 and 1989.

Panama has always been a peace-loving nation regardless of its government. Its aggressive capability on the battlefield, against any nation, is completely nonexistent, much less against the United States. Any claim to the contrary is ridiculous and an insult to normal intelligence.

On April 6, 1989, President George Bush notified Congress that he had invoked the National Emergencies Act and the international laws necessary to declare "a state of national emergency" in the United States for the special and extraordinary threat to the national security, etc., etc.

On March 2, 1988, Bush implemented measures of economic warfare against Panama.

On May 17, 1989, Bush told the *Washington Times* that he had given orders to the Pentagon to prepare for a confrontation with the Panama Defense Forces.

On May 18, a story in the *Washington Post* mentions orders to put the Defense Forces to the test by threatening to have armed U.S. convoys "poking through every hole in the wall in the houses and buildings of Panama City."

In response, Panama—its Assembly of Community Representatives, its Armed Forces, its government—continually accused the United States of acting as a menacing and invasive power and saw the necessity of protecting itself and maintaining a state of alert against these actions.

The U.S. government officials who are functioning, physically, within the offices of the government in Panama imposed by the United States are a demonstration of the domination of the weak by the strong, as well as of its true interest in keeping Panama as a robot obeying the orders of Washington. This also confirms the motives for the invasion.

The attack by the North against the social and material achievements of the Torrijos period as well as those of the Noriega period in professionalizing the Defense Forces is the proof of the need felt by the United States to wipe out any patriotic, nationalist consciousness so that the youth will have neither leaders nor stimulus in 1999, when the Canal is supposed to revert to Panamanian control and the last foreign soldier is to leave Panamanian soil. That is to say, they wish to brainwash and purge the Panamanian soul of any yearning for economic, military and political liberation.

With the imposition of the new government, there has been a return to the origins of the republic and the return of those who ruled from 1904 until 1968 as a wealthy social class, under whose rule the children of the marginalized and the poor had no opportunities. They have now been returned to that same, old-style politics; now the leading positions are in the hands of other social classes and groupings who have their own idea of social justice.

Resolution of the Organization
of American States

*The following resolution, #534 (800/89),
was adopted by the Organization of
American States on December 22, 1989.*

Serious Events in the Republic of Panama

THE PERMANENT COUNCIL OF THE ORGANIZATION OF AMERICAN
STATES HAVING SEEN:

The serious events in the Republic of Panama, especially the armed
clashes resulting from the military intervention by the United States and
the deplorable loss of lives and property;

The obligation of States not to intervene, directly or indirectly, for any
reason whatever, in the internal or external affairs of any other State,
and

The obligation to respect the inviolability of the territory of a State,
which may not be the object, even temporarily, of military occupation or
of other measures of force taken by another State, directly or indirectly,
on any grounds whatever, and

CONSIDERING:

The provisions of resolution I adopted by the Twenty-first Meeting of
Consultation of Ministers of Foreign Affairs on May 17, 1989 and the
declarations made by the President of the Meeting and adopted on June
6, July 20, and August 24, 1989 on the Panamanian crisis in its international context;

That, at its nineteenth regular session, the General Assembly requested
the Permanent Council to keep the situation in Panama under permanent
consideration;

That any just and lasting solution to the Panamanian problem must be
based upon full respect for the right of its people to self-determination
without outside interference;

124

That it is necessary to guarantee full respect for the sovereignty of Panama;

That it is also necessary to reestablish conditions that will guarantee the full exercise of the human rights and fundamental freedoms of the Panamanian people;

That the Panamanian people have the inalienable right to self-determination without internal dictates or external interference,

RESOLVES:

1. To deeply regret the military intervention in Panama.

2. To urge the immediate cessation of hostilities and bloodshed and to request the launching of negotiations between the various political sectors of the country that will lead to a concerted solution to the Panamanian institutional crisis.

3. To express its deepest concern over the serious incidents and the loss of lives taking place in the Republic of Panama.

4. To call for the withdrawal of the foreign troops used for the military intervention and to reaffirm that solving the crisis Panama is undergoing at this time necessarily requires full respect for the right of the Panamanian people to self-determination without outside interference and faithful adherence to the letter and spirit of the Torrijos-Carter treaties.

5. To express the need to comply with the obligations assumed by the States in the Vienna Conventions on Diplomatic and Consular Relations.

6. To urge that the International Committee of the Red Cross (ICRC) be provided with the facilities and cooperation necessary for it to carry out its humanitarian work with the wounded and the civilian population.

7. To express its fraternal support for and solidarity with the Panamanian people and to urge that the parties involved engage in dialogue for the purpose of safeguarding the lives and personal safety of all the inhabitants of Panama.

8. To recommend that a new session of the Twenty-first Meeting of Consultation of Ministers of Foreign Affairs be held when appropriate to examine the Panamanian situation as a whole.

9. To instruct the Secretary General of the OAS to take the steps necessary for the implementation of this resolution.

The Essence of Our Movement
Is Being Tested in Panama

From a speech delivered by General of the
Army Raúl Castro Ruz, First Vice President
of the Councils of State and of Ministers of
Cuba, at the 9th Summit of Non-Aligned
Countries in Belgrade, Yugoslavia, on
September 9, 1989.

We are living in a period of enormous tension in our region. In the past weeks, accompanying an escalation of military provocations and pressures of all kinds, the risk has become imminent that the United States undertake direct aggression against Panama from the enclaves it occupies in the so-called Canal Zone.

It is therefore indispensable to closely follow the course of events, anticipate and denounce the dangers and increase our political and moral solidarity, because we live in an overheated and profoundly interconnected region. Panama is not present in this room, but its fraternal and combative message is here with us, as is the urgent call our country would like to make at this moment.

For that reason Cuba believes that its first words here should be spoken in solidarity with Panama. We believe that if this Summit is going to distinguish itself for its loyalty to the original principles of the Non-Aligned Movement, it is indispensable for our voice to be raised in defense of the self-determination of the Panamanian people.

The juncture is extremely dangerous. The United States is running an intense campaign to slander Panama and is trying to show, once more, that it is capable of manipulating events and imposing on the world what suits its interests.

The international public opinion must realize that what is at stake there is in reality the desire of the United States to break the Canal Treaties and

126

not relinquish authority over the Canal to a government which is a legitimate follower of the aspirations of General Torrijos. The crisis which is gripping Panama today is a result of interference, economic blockade, pressure and destabilization brutally and openly carried out by the U.S. government.

Panama is a worthy member of our Movement. Its demand for sovereignty over the Canal and over the territory occupied by the United States, its demand that the U.S. military bases there be dismantled, and its determination to achieve these objectives through negotiations made the Panamanian cause one which the Non-Aligned Movement has always most supported. Aggression by the United States against this small Third World country is a crime we cannot tolerate.

Today the line that puts to the test the essence of non-alignment runs through Panama. If the imperialists trample on those principles, all those here will be less independent and more vulnerable. The heroic Panamanian people must feel that they are not alone in this challenge, and that the Movement supports them without reserve in their sovereign right to solve their own problems.

We're Up Against Tremendous Odds

*The following excerpts are from a
fund-raising letter sent out by Ronald
Reagan in 1977, when Omar Torrijos was
President of Panama. Reagan held no public
office at that time but was so "worried"
about the Panama Canal Treaties (which he
said he had read "cover to cover") that he
was mustering a campaign chest to defeat
them.*

Ronald Reagan
Washington, D.C. 20013

Dear Friend and Contributor:

I need your immediate help to prevent our country from making one of the most serious mistakes in its 200 year history.

Right now, as I write this letter to you, Mr. Carter and his White House lobbyists are trying to stampede the U.S. Senate into quick ratification of the Panama Canal Treaty.

Unless you and I act now, one of the most vital shipping and defense waterways will be in the complete control of the anti-American, pro-Marxist dictator, General Torrijos.

You and I just can't let that happen. Too much is at stake. That's why I felt it was important that I alert you personally to what's been going on behind your back.

I've read this treaty carefully from cover to cover. And in my honest opinion, it's a line by line blueprint for potential disaster for our country.

That's why, in a special meeting in New Orleans, the Republican

National Committee formally adopted a resolution to oppose ratification of the Carter-negotiated Panama Canal Treaty by the U.S. Senate.

Here's why I am so worried:

1) Once the treaty is ratified, the U.S. can't build a new sea-level canal in or out of Panama without the express written permission of the Panamanian government. In the process of giving up our Canal, Mr. Carter has also surrendered our rights to build a new one if needed.

2) Once ratified, there's no guarantee our Naval Fleet will have the right of priority passage in time of war. Our Navy depends on safe, secure, unrestricted passage through the Canal. But if we lose this short-cut from the Atlantic to the Pacific, we'll lose the flexibility and quick response we need to protect our country and our holdings.

3) Once ratified, there is no guarantee the U.S. can intervene to protect and defend the neutrality of the Canal. Despite the way Mr. Carter "interprets" the treaty, Panamanian's [sic] chief negotiator, Mr. Betancourt [sic], says, flat out, "The U.S. does NOT have the right to intervene to defend the Canal."

4) Once ratified, we must close down 10 of our military bases, Americans in the Zone will be under Panamanian rule, and we must pay Torrijos millions more each year for the Canal.

... Believe me, I am counting on you to give me all the help you possibly can to defeat those who time and time again vote to weaken our national security.

... That means we must raise a minimum of $2 million.

Unless these funds are raised, we won't defeat those Democrats who vote time and time again to support actions that weaken our national security. And we will not be able to elect candidates who will stand up and support a strong U.S. foreign policy and a strong national defense.

That's exactly why your contribution is so important.

Believe me, without your support, the Canal is as good as gone. Then we'll have to write off the Canal like we were forced to write off Vietnam, Cambodia and Laos. So please, I urge you to do the following today:

Please send the most generous contribution you feel you can afford to finance this campaign. It's difficult for me to suggest a specific amount, but I know it will take many contributions of $15, $25, and $50 to win!

If you agree with me, then sign the enclosed endorsement petition and mail it back to me in the special reply envelope I have enclosed for you.

This is one of the most important battles you and I will ever fight. We're up against tremendous odds. But we can't sit back and do nothing.

It's time you and I counter the slick propaganda campaign that says our ownership of the Canal is "imperialistic." Nothing could be further from the truth.

We haven't made a nickel on the Canal. We've run it for the benefit of the entire world. And we've poured over $200 million a year into the Panamanian economy.

This debate concerns our national security. And that shouldn't be sacrificed to score a few political points with a regime in Panama that so blatantly violates the human rights of its own people.

With so much at stake, I urge you to send me your contribution so we can defeat those who vote time and time again against a strong U.S. foreign policy. ...

With deep concern,

Ronald Reagan

Chronology

The following outline of events relevant to United States-Panama relations is adapted from a chronology by Jane Franklin with the permission of the author.

1856-1989: On at least 16 occasions, United States intervenes militarily in Panama. From 1903 U.S. troops are permanently stationed there. Majority of invasions, which involve sending additional troops and weaponry, are carried out to suppress insurrections and to retain property United States had seized in Panama.

1903: U.S. show of military force in Panama accelerates its struggle to break away from Colombia. Treaty to build Panama Canal is "negotiated" and signed in United States by French businessman "representing" Panama.

1914: Panama Canal opens. United States takes control of 10-mile-wide zone in middle of country. Segregation imposed in Canal Zone against nonwhites. U.S. employees receive wages twice those of Panamanians.

1958: After popular protest, United States agrees to fly both U.S. and Panamanian flags in Canal Zone.

1959: Panamanians march into Canal Zone to raise Panamanian flag on Independence Day, are turned back by U.S. troops.

1964: Panamanians march into Zone on January 9 after U.S. students raise only U.S. flag. U.S. troops kill more than 20 Panamanian civilians and wound more than 300. Panama breaks diplomatic relations with United States. Relations resume after United States agrees to discuss new treaty.

1968: Col. Omar Torrijos overthrows government of wealthy landowners and becomes head of more nationalist military government. Period of reforms begins with expansion of literacy, education, health, rural development, trade union organization and wage laws. Blacks, Mestizos and Indians are appointed to government positions for first time. General Manuel Antonio Noriega becomes head of armed forces.

1972: Ruling Junta is confirmed by election.

1977: Three treaties known as Torrijos-Carter treaties are signed. Key provisions include total return of U.S. military bases and Canal Zone to Panama by year 2000; no interference in Panama's internal affairs; and restrictions on U.S. military presence in Panama.

1979: Treaties take effect; 65% of the Zone reverts to Panamanian control.

1980: Ronald Reagan campaigns for President with promise not to give up Canal.

1981: General Torrijos is killed in airplane crash.

1983: General Noriega is named Commander of newly created Panamanian Defense Forces.

1985: Relations between Noriega and United States become hostile after Panama rebuffs demands of Admiral Poindexter, Reagan's National Security Adviser, to collaborate on invasion of Nicaragua.

1986: U.S. government proposes turning over Canal by 1990 if agreement is reached to allow U.S. bases to remain until 2015.

September 24, 1987: U.S. Senate approves resolution demanding that Panama change its government or face a cutoff of U.S. aid.

February 4, 1988: Noriega is indicted by Federal grand juries in Miami and Tampa on drug trafficking.

February 8, 1988: Noriega demands withdrawal of U.S. Southern Command headquartered in Panama.

February 26, 1988: National Assembly (the Congress of Panama) blocks move by President Delvalle to remove General Noriega. Delvalle is removed for violating Panamanian Constitution (similar to impeachment). Washington continues to recognize Delvalle as President after National Assembly names Solís Palma as Acting President.

March 11, 1988: Reagan Administration imposes sanctions, including restrictions on trade and withholding of Canal fees.

April 1988: Reagan Administration increases economic sanctions. U.S. government and private U.S. companies are prohibited from making payments to Panama; $56 million in Panamanian funds in U.S. banks frozen; United States sends additional 2,000 troops to Panama in violation of 1977 treaties. United States gives $10 million to Guillermo Endara as presidential candidate. Many more millions are reported to be given covertly. (U.S. election law bars candidates from receiving foreign contributions.)

May 25, 1988: U.S. Secretary of State George Shultz announces talks on deal for Noriega's departure have collapsed.

May 7, 1989: Presidential election takes place. Panamanian government nullifies results on May 10 because of U.S. interference. Bush Administration sends 2,000 more troops to Panama. U.S. military starts staging regular military maneuvers on Panamanian territory in violation of treaties. Over 100 such acts take place. Panama appeals to United Nations for observers and assistance in stopping U.S. military activity.

May 11, 1989: President Bush recalls Ambassador Arthur Davis. Begins sending additional 1,700 soldiers and 165 Marines to Panama.

June 1989: U.S. Justice Department issues opinion that United States can carry out arrests in foreign countries without approval of their governments.

September 12, 1989: Bush Administration again expands sanctions, including withdrawing 1989 sugar quota and adding to list of companies and individuals barred from doing business with U.S. citizens and traveling to United States.

October 3, 1989: Noriega puts down coup attempt supported by U.S. government.

October 17, 1989: Bush Administration supports wider role for CIA in coup attempts, complaining that restraints about possible death of targets is too limiting.

November 1989: U.S. government announces that after January 31, 1990, it will bar vessels registered in Panama from entering U.S. ports. This forces other countries to pressure the Panamanian government, as majority of countries in world use Panamanian registry for commercial vessels.

December 20, 1989: United States invades Panama.

Voices from Panama meeting, April 5, 1990, at Town Hall in New York City, organized by the Independent Commission of Inquiry on the U.S. Invasion of Panama.
(Photos: George Ives, Haïti Progrès, New York)

Carl Glenn

Afterword

Carl Glenn, a staff member of the
Commission of Inquiry, made two
investigative visits to Panama after
the invasion, first in February/March
1990 and again in August 1991.

There weren't many people present in the U.S. Senate chamber on the afternoon of Thursday, July 25, 1991. Nothing was visible to suggest anything but an ordinary Washington scene. Yet thousands of Panamanian children, women and men had perished in blood and fire on Christmas Eve 19 months earlier to make this Senate session possible.

Some present appeared bored and impatient. One senator took the floor to complain that nobody was there. "We could finish this bill sometime today if we will combat our nocturnal tendencies and try to work during the day... " he said.

Larry Craig, senator from Idaho, then took the floor.

"I am offering an amendment," he stated, "which expresses the sense of the Senate that the President should seek to negotiate a new base rights agreement with Panama to allow United States troops to remain in Panama beyond December 31, 1999.

"It also states," he went on, "that the troops should retain the ability to act independently to protect U.S. interests and the operation of the Canal."

The amendment declared that "the Republic of Panama has dissolved its defense forces and has no standing army, or other defense forces, capable of defending the Panama Canal from aggressors, and therefore, remains vulnerable to attack from both inside and outside of Panama and this may impair or interrupt the operation and accessibility of the Panama Canal; the presence of the United States Armed Forces offers the best defense against sabotage. ..." It finally called on the President to negotiate a new agreement "to allow the permanent stationing of United States military forces in Panama beyond December 31, 1999."[1]

---

1. The ammendment was part of the International Security and Economic Cooperation Act of 1991 (S. 1435), "to ammend the Foreign Assistance Act of 1961 and the Arms Export and Control Act, and related statutory provisions... ." The *Congressional Record — Senate,* July 25, 1991.

The amendment was then adopted by the senators present.

This maneuver was carried out deep in the marble caverns of the Capitol and reported nowhere beyond the Congressional Record. The Independent Commission of Inquiry undertook to investigate and report on the crimes committed during the U.S. invasion of Panama because of the conspiracy of silence, as we referred to it at the time, in which the events were cloaked.

The White House and Pentagon version of events has gone virtually unchallenged in Congress. A few questions have been raised in the House but they have remained unanswered.

The real purpose behind the U.S. invasion of Panama was to crush the independence of this small but strategically important Central American republic and reduce it to a *de facto* U.S. protectorate.

As we pointed out, the U.S. refusal to abide by the terms of the Canal Treaties was central to their motives. The invasion was launched 11 days before Panama was to exercise effective control over the Canal for the first time by the shift of the majority of Canal Commission members from U.S. to Panamanian citizens.[2]

At the same time that the Senate was adopting the amendment mentioned above (a virtually identical amendment was also inserted by the Senate into the Defense Authorization Act on August 2), hearings were being held in the House of Representatives. On July 17 and July 30 witnesses testified before the House Subcommittee on Western Hemisphere Affairs of the Foreign Affairs Committee.

These hearings were not linked to any legislation. They were held for the purpose of orienting Congress to the situation in Panama from the point of view of the Pentagon and the State Department. None of the witnesses presented in this book were invited to describe the disastrous changes experienced by the Panamanian people since the invasion. No native Panamanian was invited to speak at all. The tone adopted during the first of these hearings, however, was cautionary.[3]

The hearings were called, "Post-Invasion Panama: Status of Democracy and the Civilian Casualty Controversy." Their second part focused largely

2. *Panama Canal Treaty,* Article III, Canal Operation and Management 3.(C).
3. The five witnesses heard at the July 17 hearing were: Prof. Richard Millet of the University of Southern Illinois; Malcolm McConnell, described in his statement as "journalist and author"; Eva Loser, Fellow, Americas Program, Center for Strategic and International Studies; David Nachman, member of Board of Directors of Americas Watch, who concluded his remarks with the comment that "in El Chorrillo, inadequate observance of the rule of proportionality [between civilian and military casualties of war] resulted in unacceptable civilian deaths and destruction"; and Richard Koster, co-author of *Time of the Tyrants: Panama 1968-1989.* Koster, who first went to Panama stationed with what was to become the 470th Military Intelligence Brigade, has lived in Panama since 1957.
The July 30 session heard only Bernard Aronson, Assistant Secretary of State for Inter-American Affairs, and Brig. Gen. James R. Harding, Director, Inter-American Region Office of the Deputy Assistant Secretary of Defense (Inter-American Affairs).

on the number of civilian deaths. Brig. Gen. James R. Harding, director of the Inter-American Region Office of the Secretary of Defense, focused most of his testimony on an effort to minimize the number of Panamanians butchered by the invading army.

The Independent Commission of Inquiry continues to maintain that thousands were killed. All of the evidence untainted by the desire of the White House and the Pentagon to hide their crimes points to this conclusion. We hold to the importance of this question for precisely the same reason that the Pentagon wants to bury it.

The attitude of the White House and the Pentagon toward the question of casualties in the Gulf War against Iraq, just a year later, is highly relevant. On March 21, 1991, the United Nations, accomplice to the U.S. aggression, issued its famous report calling the destruction of civilian life in Iraq "near apocalyptic."

Although the Pentagon refused to provide an estimate of the number of Iraqis killed, U.S. military officials in Riyadh, Saudi Arabia, were quoted at that time by the Associated Press as estimating the total Iraqi dead at 100,000. Other independent estimates were much higher. In addition, the UN report stated that the U.S. bombing had left some 72,000 people homeless, that 90% of Iraq's industrial workers were "reduced to inactivity" and that most families lacked "access to adequate rations or the purchasing power to meet normal minimal standards."

The following day, when asked about the number of Iraqis killed, the Chairman of the Joint Chiefs of Staff, Colin Powell, replied, "It's really not a number I'm terribly interested in." Excerpts from this interview were published in *The New York Times* on March 23. The bluntness of this remark was a product of the drunken triumphalism of the moment. But the political substance was a product of the impunity that the Pentagon felt especially after the collapse of the socialist countries in Eastern Europe enabled Washington to get UN endorsement for its attack.

"How to Be the World's Policeman" was published in the *The New York Times Magazine* in May, 1991, authored by Col. Harry G. Summers, U.S. Army, ret., a "distinguished fellow" at the Army War College. The colonel said that, "When the Iron Curtain crumbled in November 1989 ... the United States was no longer constrained by fear of a nuclear confrontation with the Soviet Union and could wield its military power in a way not possible since World War II. ... Like it or not, a New World Order is at hand in which much of the world seems to be teetering on the edge of anarchy and the United States...finds itself liable to be forced into the role of the world's policeman."

For the purposes of our investigation, the most important part of this remarkable statement is the date cited by the author. It was November 1989, just a month prior to the invasion of Panama, that the United States felt "no longer constrained."

But the contrast from the defiant and dismissive tone of Gen. Powell's comment to the defensive and confused accounting offered to Congress by Gen. Harding in connection with the death toll of Panamanians as a result of the invasion is instructive.

When Gen. Harding testified on July 30, 1991, before the House sub-committee, his assignment was to put an end to the controversy on the question of civilian casualties.

"The bottom-line, Mr. Chairman, is that there was no 'cover-up'; casualties were in the range reported and USSOUTHCOM remains open to assist the Government of Panama in any further developments in these matters," were the general's concluding words.

Let us examine this statement. The general was exaggerating his powers by claiming to be in a position to draw the "bottom line" on this question. This is precisely what the Congress, the Pentagon and the White House wish they were able to do. Despite their repeated assertion, these claims have only grown more difficult to support.

Gen. Harding told the Congressional panel that the estimates of thousands of dead "are based on allegations that many Panamanian dead are buried in Panama in undiscovered common graves. However, the only common graves 'discovered' ... to date were the two already accounted for by the Institute of Legal Medicine."

In March 1990, Peter Eisner, a U.S. journalist, was shown a list of hundreds of names of people who disappeared at the time of the invasion and were still missing. These were in addition to the 570 Panamanians officially acknowledged to have been killed. This list was compiled by an office in the Public Force, the new police department in Panama established under U.S. supervision. It was based on the reports of families who had gone to the new authorities in search of their loved ones. That list has disappeared.

When Lt. Ida Aguilera de García, who was in charge of that effort, was asked in December 1990 by the same journalist how those cases had been resolved, she would say only that she had turned the list over to her superiors. Her superiors say such an accounting never took place or, if it did, they were unaware of it.[4]

Army Gen. Fred Woerner was the commander in chief of the U.S. Southern Command in Panama from June 1987 to August 1989 and instrumental in planning the invasion.

"In a society that has made almost a fetish of statistical precision, it [the lack of a U.S. death count] exacerbates the suspicions that there is something to be hidden in our failure to act consistently in Panama," Woerner, then retired, told an interviewer in December 1990.[5]

4. *New York Newsday*, Dec. 21, 1990.
5. Ibid.

A comment in a similar vein was made by Catholic Archbishop Marcos McGrath. He told reporters in an interview for a CBS "White Paper," "I feel that neither the U.S. government nor the Panamanian government are interested in finding out the truth" about the number of civilians killed in the invasion.[6]

One concrete reason motivating this suppression of the truth was uncovered by the law firm of Kiyonaga and Kiyonaga. They had undertaken a suit on behalf of families of victims of the invasion. Through the Freedom of Information Act, they obtained a memorandum written by Maj. Joseph A. Goetzke, Chief of the Special Claims Branch of the Army. This memo stated that "Payment of individual combat-related claims under a program similar to the USAID program in Grenada would not be in the best interest of the Department of Defense of the US because of the potentially huge number of such claims."[7]

An important example of how accurate information about this issue can be distorted or suppressed altogether came to light on August 12, 1991.

A delegation consisting of a representative of the El Chorrillo War Refugees Committee; Olga Mejía, president of the non-governmental National Human Rights Commission of Panama (CONADEHUPA); and Carl Glenn, a staff member of the Independent Commission of Inquiry met, with Father Javier Arteta, the Catholic priest of the church in El Chorrillo. Father Arteta has been quoted frequently in the press as an incontrovertible witness substantiating U.S. military claims on the origin of the fires in El Chorrillo, as well as the cause and the quantity of deaths in that neighborhood.

At the House subcommittee hearings on July 17, Father Arteta was cited in a prepared statement by Malcolm McConnell. McConnell is author of a book, "Just Cause—The Real Story of America's High Tech Invasion of Panama," published by St. Martin's Press in November, 1991. He was granted interviews with "key planners, commanders and participants....Overall I formed a very favorable assessment of the U.S. military planning and conduct of Operation Just Cause," he states.

Olga Mejía, who grew up in El Chorrillo and lived for two years at the Fatima church, read a translation of McConnell's statement to Father Arteta himself.

"In my opinion," read Mejía from McConnell's statement, "one of the most reliable sources on this subject [the obliteration of El Chorrillo] is Father Javier Arteta. Not only was he an eyewitness to the arson by the Dignity Battalion members, he documented the progress of the fire with his camera. His photographs show that the fire began and spread during the daylight hours of December 20, not during the night when U.S. firepower was brought to bear on the Comandancia."

---

6. Cited by Kevin Buckley in *Panama the Whole Story,* Simon & Schuster, 1991.
7. Ibid.

Father Arteta listened carefully to the reading. At the conclusion, he characterized McConnell's assertions as "lies." He said this was typical of the way his words have been twisted and he had been misquoted.

He said that he was aware of three fires. Two of them had begun during the assault on the Comandancia during the night as a direct result of U.S. firepower. The third and most destructive fire began the following morning as a result of combat between U.S. and Panamanian forces. (He repeatedly emphasized that these were the only events he was personally aware of and that he made no claim to omniscience.)

"This was a war. If the Panamanian soldiers fought back, what could they be expected to do? If someone is shooting at you, you can't fold your arms. If a fire was caused by this combat then it was a product of the war. We had been invaded," he said.

He further stated that during the months immediately following the invasion he was told on various occasions that $42 million in U.S. aid was dependent on his statements and that this would be decisive in whether or not the refugees of El Chorrillo, the members of his parish, would receive any compensation.

Finally, let us look at how the United States handled the issue of casualties in its next war. In September 1991, news reports quoted U.S. Army officers saying that Army tanks had buried alive possibly thousands of Iraqi soldiers in their trenches during the war against Iraq. On October 29, the Iraqi News Agency reported that the bodies of 44 of these soldiers were unearthed near the Saudi-Iraqi border.

"At the Pentagon," according to a brief article in the Oct. 30 New York Newsday based on combined wire-service dispatches, "Pete Williams, spokesman for Defense Secretary Dick Cheney, said U.S. officials were still weighing whether to notify the International Red Cross about locations of the graves."

Perhaps the best way to test their explanation of why it was absolutely necessary to invade Panama is to examine their handling of the trial of General Noriega. He was made the personal embodiment of every reason the U.S. gave for the invasion.

It was presumed at the time of the invasion that for the United States to embark on such a drastic action against a sovereign nation, one which violated the most fundamental principles of international law and human rights, it must have had unassailable and overwhelming evidence against General Noriega.

Just two months before the invasion, the White House, the CIA and the Department of Justice took the precaution of sending messages to Congress calling for the loosening of restrictions against the killing of a head of state during a U.S.-supported coup attempt. The new legal interpretationwould permit such an assassination to take place "in the heat of battle."[8]

Nevertheless, Noriega survived the invasion and the United States found itself in the awkward position of having to proceed with a trial. But weren't the prosecution, the Justice Department, the Pentagon and George Bush eager to see a fair and speedy trial by a jury of the peers of the accused? Was there any better way to demonstrate the fairness of the U.S. government?

In our Report we cited a June 1990 *New York Times* article in which "disappointed American officials say they have found almost no documents so far that conclusively prove General Noriega trafficked in drugs."[9]

The article reported that the *Times* had conducted a highly unusual investigation of its own. "In an effort to assess the Government's case against General Noriega, interviews with more than 15 current and former American intelligence officials, as well as several former members of the Panamanian Government, were carried out in four countries.

"... A six-month review of tens of thousands of captured documents has turned up no evidence of drug dealing by General Noriega, according to three American officials closely informed of the painstaking review of documents by several American agencies. ... 'We've found no smoking gun in the documents,' said an American official in Panama."

Noriega's defense attorney, Frank Rubino, suggested in an interview at the time that U.S. intelligence agencies sifting through these documents were also taking the opportunity to "sanitize" them of any evidence demonstrating their own role in drug trafficking into the U.S.[10]

Two weeks after Noriega was taken from the Vatican Embassy in Panama City to a jail cell in Miami, his lawyers filed a motion with a U.S. magistrate barring the government from destroying any documents belonging to the general that were confiscated in the invasion. The magistrate, William C. Turnoff, also ordered the government to list everything taken from General Noriega's home and military offices.

Evidence has come to light since the invasion suggesting that instead of the touted "war on drugs," the U.S. government may actually be protecting the cocaine industry. The defense contends that Manuel Noriega acted as an employee of a variety of U.S. government agencies in this "war." Evidence continues to accumulate of the participation of top members of the U.S.-installed government of Panama in the drug trade.

And there is another side to this explosive issue. U.S. banks are in crisis. So many of them have failed that the Federal Deposit Insurance Corporation is on the verge of insolvency. The U.S. Treasury has already disgorged

8. *The New York Times,* Oct. 17, 18; Nov. 4, 5, 1989.
9. *The New York Times,* June 10, 1990.
10. Ibid.

hundreds of billions of dollars to "bail out" the savings and loans institutions. Meanwhile, drug exports are the largest single source of income for some Latin American countries that owe hundreds of billions of dollars to U.S. and other banks. The debt service these countries must pay may be crucial to these banks' survival. Moreover, the deposits and money-laundering operations are a source of income to these same banks.

The administration's "war on drugs" came in for harsh criticism on April 13, 1989, when the Senate Foreign Relations subcommittee on narcotics, terrorism and international operations issued a report concluding a two-year investigation. "Other foreign policy interests were permitted to sidetrack, disrupt and undercut the war on drugs," Senator John Kerry, chair of the subcommittee told a press conference.

According to *The New York Times,* "Committee investigators said their inquiry was hindered by uncooperative Federal officials. The report itself quotes Jeffrey Feldman, a former United States Attorney in Miami, as having said Justice Department officials told him that representatives of the department, Drug Enforcement Administration and Federal Bureau of Investigation met in 1986 'to discuss how Senator Kerry's efforts' to push for hearings 'could be undermined.'"[11]

The principal investigator for the report, Jack A. Blum, said the findings showed that "the real contra-drug story is that we simply did not crack down on people that were doing us a favor."[12]

Among the specific examples cited in the Senate report were State Department payments of $806,401 between January and August 1986 to four companies "owned and operated by narcotics traffickers" to carry supplies to the contra mercenary army. It was just eight months after the release of this report that the Bush administration launched its high-tech invasion of Panama—and the best excuse they could come up with was to depict General Noriega as a drug trafficker.

In 1990, upon his retirement, top DEA undercover officer Michael Levine stated in his book *Deep Cover,* "It is both sobering and painful to realize, after twenty-five years of undercover work, having personally accounted for at least three thousand criminals serving fifteen thousand years in jail, and having seized several tons of illegal substances, that my career was meaningless and had had absolutely no effect whatsoever in the so-called war on drugs. The war itself was a fraud."

He recounts his participation in a sting operation which involved the infiltration of a Bolivian coca-paste producing corporation. He describes conducting the investigation against the determined opposition of the DEA hierarchy. In the end, 854 pounds of cocaine base were seized and two of

11. *The New York Times,* April 14, 1989.
12. Ibid.

the most powerful drug dealers in history were arrested after accepting a payment of $9 million in a Miami bank vault.

"Instead of our government pursuing the investigation and its implications with all its resources, strange things started to happen. All charges were dropped against one of the two defendants and the bail of the other was mysteriously lowered, after which he was allowed to leave the United States without the slightest hindrance by our government."

In a radio interview broadcast in New York on November 11, 1991, Levine identified the Federal prosecutor responsible for the release of these two individuals as Michael P. Sullivan, who by that time was acting as lead prosecutor in the trial of General Noriega.[13]

It took nearly two years for the U.S. government to bring Noriega to trial. During this time a pattern of disruption aimed at the defense emerged. Shortly before the trial began, it was learned that Raymond Takiff, Gen. Noriega's chief defense attorney until the general's abduction from Panama, was working as an undercover informant for the U.S. Attorney's office in Miami. It was Takiff who, while Noriega sought asylum at the Vatican Embassy in Panama City, urged him to surrender to U.S. forces. When this was reported in the press, the prosecution said they had done nothing improper. Their excuse was that the sanctity of the client-attorney relationship did not apply until Gen. Noriega entered U.S. jurisdiction. In a pre-trial action which gave the proceedings a further Alice-in-Wonderland quality, Judge William Hoeveler ruled that because Noriega was not a U.S. citizen and was not in the United States at the time, he had no constitutional protections against unreasonable searches and seizures!

This question of the supposedly protected nature of attorney-client communications again became an issue when tape recordings by the government of conversations between the general and his lawyers were circulated and then broadcast over radio and TV. In court papers filed in Miami on December 7, 1990, the prosecution admitted having taped more than 1,400 telephone conversations, many of them between Gen. Noriega and his lawyers.[14]

Then, after an explicit ban by Judge Hoeveler, the defense witness list was placed in the hands of the prosecutors. A federal marshal assigned to deliver the subpoenas to witnesses on the list "accidentally" gave the list to Lewis Tambs, former U.S. ambassador to Costa Rica, who sent it to the State Department— even though a copy of the judge's banning order was attached—and they sent it to the Justice Department who made sure that the prosecution got a copy. The disclosure of the list is damaging to the defense in a federal case because the defense is barred from seeing the prosecution witness list.

---

13. Paul DeRienzo interview with Michael Levine, on "Undercurrents," on WBAI-FM, New York.
14. *The New York Times,* Dec. 8, 1990.

Earlier, the government had prevented the defense attorneys from receiving any of General Noriega's money. This was not simply a case of lawyers having to work without pay. It raised an enormous barrier preventing the accused, who is still presumed innocent under the U.S. Constitution, from being able to mount an effective defense. While this ban was finally lifted, the judge ruled inadmissable evidence to prove the U.S. government's own role in drug trafficking. He cited "national security" and the need to prevent the defense from "politicizing" the trial. Nevertheless, as a result of this dispute, the government was forced to admit for the first time that Gen. Noriega had indeed been on the U.S. government payroll.

However, the most flagrant subversion of even the pretense of justice are the cash payoffs and other incentives given by the government to prosecution witnesses for their testimony. For example, there is the case of Carlos Lehder, a former leading figure in the Medellin, Colombia cocaine monopoly. He was serving a life-plus-130-year sentence in the maximum security wing of the Marion, Illinois federal penitentiary. Since his conviction for drug trafficking in 1988 he has been in solitary confinement, with no hope of ever being released. In exchange for his testimony, federal authorities granted him: an immediate suspension of his life sentence; the possibility of release on parole; the immediate concession of visas to his family to move to the United States where they would receive federal protection, and more.[15]

Max Mermelstein, a convicted drug smuggler and employee of the Medellín Cartel who testified during the opening days of the trial, received $670,000 (as of October 1991) for his testimony. Nor did Mermelstein have to enter the federal witness protection program alone. According to government attorneys, Mermelstein was accompanied into witness protection by 17 of his family members.[16] The total monetary payments to government witnesses have exceeded $1.5 million.

Noriega attorney Frank Rubino told a National Public Radio interviewer that if he were to buy a witness a cup of coffee, he would be accused by the government of obstruction of justice. A federal judge in Kansas City, Missouri, who was prevented from reducing the sentence of a man convicted in a drug-related case said, "If they can do what they're doing down there in the trial of Noriega, they ought to be able to do something here." Although public criticism by one judge of another is rare, U.S. District Judge Scott O. Wright couldn't suppress his outrage: "I mean they're cutting deals down there that are obscene."[17]

On September 4, 1991, the opening day of the trial, the former chair of the criminal law division of the Association of Trial Lawyers of America, Joseph Lawless, said of the general's prosecutors: "They've shown more

15. *El Diario/La Prensa,* Sept. 26, 1991.

16. *El Diario/La Prensa,* Sept. 19, 1991.

17. *The Washington Post,* Oct. 5, 1991.

contempt for Noriega's Constitutional rights than any other criminal defendant I can think of."[18]

The June 1990 *New York Times* article summed up the predicament of those behind the invasion in the following terms: "The government is...forced to justify invading Panama and killing more than 200 civilians to arrest a man the American government helped train, support and maintain.

"It also appears possible that even if the Government wins its case, the conviction may be for drug dealing that is relatively small scale by Latin American standards... In contrast, American officials strongly suspect high-ranking military officers in Honduras, Guatemala and El Salvador of similar, and in some cases even greater involvement in drug dealing—yet have not taken harsh action against them."

Finally it quotes a Justice Department official involved in the case, "...this is a case the government can't afford to lose."[19]

Rather than swarm to Miami to report on this utterly unique and unprecedented trial, the media have stayed away in droves. Even as it began, the trial became a non-story, receiving scant coverage when it was mentioned at all. Still less is reported in the U.S. media about the state of affairs in Panama.

In our report, we detailed the spurious nature of the Endara regime, with State Department and Pentagon proconsuls directing every government office. Guillermo Endara, the titular head of state, is the object of open ridicule. Recent polls rate him as the least popular public figure in the country, with an "approval rating" of 15%.

Following the invasion, Bush named Deane Hinton U.S. ambassador to Panama. Ambassador Hinton began his long career at the State Department in Washington in 1946. From 1967 to 1969 he headed the Agency for International Development (AID) office in Guatemala.

Through semi-autonomous "Public Safety Programs," AID was the principal organizer of the activities described by Philip Agee at the beginning of this book. There is abundant documented evidence of the role of the CIA in financing and directing these police programs. They had the aim of developing "investigative mechanisms capable of detecting subversive individuals and organizations, collecting and collating information relative to their activities and neutralizing their efforts."[20]

Assistant Secretary of State Alexis Johnson described the strategy and tactics formulated during the 1960s by the State Department and the

---

18. *USA Today*, Sept. 4, 1991.
19. *The New York Times*, Dec. 8, 1990.
20. From a 1962 Ad Hoc Interagency commission study quoted in M. McClintock, *The American Connection, Volume I: State Terror and Popular Resistance in El Salvador*, Zed Books, 1985. Nearly identical language is used in an AID/Office of Public Safety report, *AID Assistance to Civil Security Forces* presented to the Senate Foreign Relations Committee in February, 1967.

Pentagon. It was "no longer possible to make a division between the activities related to the waging of war and diplomatic activities," he said in a graduation speech at the Inter-American Defense College in 1966. "One must weigh concrete military measures in terms of their political impact and vice versa."[21]

The number of extra-judicial executions and political assassinations carried out as part of the "pacification" programs conducted during the period of Hinton's tenure with AID in Guatemala and later as ambassador to El Salvador (1981-1983) were particularly high. Between these two assignments Hinton was employed by AID in Chile during the first years of Salvador Allende's socialist Popular Unity government (1969-1971).

In the late '60s and early '70s an elaborate telecommunications system was installed throughout Central America with all channels terminating at the U.S. Southern Command headquarters in Panama. This network, continually upgraded, was first set up under the auspices of the Office of Public Safety of AID. However, U.S. Southern Command commander in chief General Porter told the House Foreign Affairs Committee in 1966 that military communications assistance in the region was designed to mesh with civilian security assistance in order to ensure "effective national and regional military command and control systems for support of counterinsurgency operations."[22]

The CIA and the Office of Public Safety of AID set up an office for "national security" within the office of the president in Guatemala in the 1960s. In December of 1990 it was reported for the first time that a similar office had been set up in the President's office in Panama almost immediately after the invasion.[23] In the storm of controversy that developed in the Panamanian press following this revelation, Endara defended the existence of this secret agency, comprised of 100 operatives. The secret operation was being paid for entirely by the U.S. treasury. It receives no money from the Panamanian government and has no Panamanian oversight.

Leaders of the opposition have become targets of repression, objects of what has come to be known in Panama as "judicial terror." Professor Cecilio Simón, the former dean of the School of Public Administration, the first Black to be elected to that post, was framed on false criminal charges and is in hiding. Professor Simón, whose testimony appears in this book has been one of the most effective in reaching out internationally, presenting evidence of Panamanian realities . He has played a critical role in the investigation of the Independent Commission of Inquiry.

---

21. Ibid.
22. Ibid.
23. David Adams, reporting from Panama City on Dec. 25, 1990 on National Public Radio's "Morning Edition."

Juan McKenzie is president of the National Council of Fired Workers (CONADE), which has organized the thousands of people fired from their jobs in the wake of the invasion. This organization is planning to broaden its scope to represent all of the unemployed. A large proportion of those fired after the invasion had their names placed on a list, circulated among employers, preventing them from finding any kind of work. McKenzie, an electronics engineer, was fired from his job at the government-owned telephone company. He was arrested by the 470th Military Intelligence Brigade of the U.S. Southern Command, according to reports that were later denied by Panamanian government authorities.[24] He was initially held on the charge of "impersonating a police officer," an accusation that was subsequently abandoned. He was then charged with "threatening the integrity of the State," on the sole basis of a leaflet he had in his pocket which he had been handed at a street demonstration.

In August 1991, the Independent Commission of Inquiry met with families of political prisoners who were arrested during the invasion and were still being held 20 months later, many still not charged with any crime. Panama, like the United States, legally recognizes the presumption of innocence. On the rare occasions when, for lack of any legal case against them, judges ordered the release (under high bail and condition of house arrest) of military or civilian leaders held since the invasion, the judges were summarily fired.

Judge Guillermo Salazar was fired in February 1991, after ordering the release under house arrest of Carlos Villalaz, the former attorney general of Panama. Judge Luis Guillermo Zúñiga who had been appointed to replace Judge Salazar, was fired in August 1991 after ordering the release on bail of Marco Justine and Rafael Cedeno, both former Panama Defense Force colonels. Endara denounced the decisions of both judges in comments widely reported on radio and TV. José A. Alvarez, president of the Panama National Bar Association, pointed out that the authority to separate judges from their posts, according to the Panamanian constitution, rests solely with the Judicial Council, which played no part in either firing. Alvarez characterized the firing of Zúñiga as part of the "climate of judicial terror" motivated by political considerations.[25]

But as the overt and covert agents of U.S. domination have tightened their grip, drug trafficking through Panama has flourished. Panama has become "even more of a land of opportunity for drug traffickers" than it was before the invasion. These are the words of Charles Rangel, the Congressional

---

24. *La Prensa* of Panama, July 5, 1991. McKenzie's interrogation at the hands of the 470th Military Intelligence Brigade was corroborated in a report prepared by the Center for Panamanian Political Studies (CEPPA), "Estudio de Casos de Presos Políticos en Panamá."
25. *La Estrella de Panamá*, August 9, 1991.

representative from Harlem and Chair of the House Select Committee on Narcotics Abuse and Control. On July 22, 1991, Rangel released a Government Accounting Office report that cites DEA estimates that the drug commerce and money laundering through Panama may have doubled since "Operation Just Cause."[26]

Although the report confirmed State Department "concerns" expressed earlier in their annual anti-narcotics study, Bernard Aronson, Assistant Secretary of State for Inter-American Affairs, was defensive. "They didn't know how much [drug] trafficking was going on before the invasion," he told reporters, "and we don't know what it is now."[27]

An article that appeared on the front page of the The New York Times three weeks later suggested that surging cocaine traffic through Panama justified further U.S. intervention. "[The increased drug traffic] is partly the result of a decision by the civilian Government to assure that the armed forces and the police do not regain the strength they enjoyed during the Noriega years."[28]

It advanced the argument that direct policing of Panama by the U.S. Armed Forces is a necessary corollary to the strengthening of "democratic institutions" within Panama. It mentioned in passing that another pact, a further infringement on Panamanian sovereignty, was signed earlier in 1991. This granted the United States the right to maintain joint patrols of Panamanian territorial waters and board and inspect commercial vessels and other craft without Panama's prior knowledge or consent.

The August 13, 1991 Times article mentioned above quoted Rodrigo Arosemena, chief of Panama's Custom Service, saying that "the truth is there are a lot of people in the system protecting and actually helping narco-traffickers."

It then went on to say that according to U.S. officials, "the Endara Government has been cooperative. But though Mr. Endara and many of his officials are lawyers and bankers familiar with the banking system, they have initiated no money-laundering investigations that were not first suggested by United States officials. Mr. Endara and his Attorney General, Rogelio Cruz, were members of the boards of banks that were shut down because of money laundering, but both deny wrongdoing."

Evidence has continued to accumulate implicating Endara personally and others around him in the cocaine business. On April 18, 1991, for example, the daily paper *El Panamá América* reported that DEA agent Ivette Torres had been transferred from an assignment to investigate firms engaged in money laundering after receiving death threats. These occurred the day

---

26. *The Washington Post,* July 23, 1991.
27. Ibid.
28. *The New York Times,* Aug. 13, 1991.

after Torres gave a sworn statement to Panamanian legislator Gerardo Gonzalez disclosing that her investigation had discovered the operation of six companies used to launder drug money. President Endara, said Torres, had been the treasurer of all six companies. Owned by Cuban-Americans, they had imported a ton of cocaine a month for the past ten years.

The U.S. military presence on the streets of Panama has continued illegally since the invasion. But on December 5, 1990, less than a year later, U.S. troops again stormed the streets of the capital armed for war. The confrontation that day was the culmination of a year of mounting popular resistance to U.S. encroachments on national sovereignty.

Demonstrations led by the trade unions, the El Chorrillo War Refugees Committee, the Association of Families of Those Who Fell December 20, the National Council of Fired Workers (CONADE), and others grew in size, frequency and confidence through September, October and November. These organizations demanded restitution for damages caused by the invasion and the restoration of jobs and democratic rights that had been lost under the occupation regime. A march was called for December 4, and a one-day work stoppage for December 5.

Separately, but concurrently, members of the new police force were organizing a job action to demand better wages and conditions. In the middle of all this, Col. Eduardo Herrera Hassan "escaped" from prison. The alleged escape was effected by helicopter from the high-security prison on the island of Naos. This prison occupies the installations formerly used by the Pentagon's Anti-Terror unit, UESAT, of Fort Amador. According to *El Panamá América*,[29] the prison has "two security cordons, one internal and one external, and two attack helicopters" standing at the ready. It is surrounded by U.S. military bases in the midst of one of the densest concentrations of sophisticated military radar and telecommunications facilities in the world.

Herrera had been hand-picked to lead the new police department formed by the occupation forces following the invasion. Replaced in August, 1990, he was subsequently accused of plotting a coup. (Herrera denied these charges and although he was outside the country at the time, he returned in an effort to prove his innocence and was arrested.) After his flight from prison, Herrera was permitted to pass from one military installation to another and was about to participate with other members of the police force in a march to air their grievances when over 500 combat-ready U.S. troops poured into the streets surrounding the police compound. In the attack that ensued, one Panamanian was shot to death by U.S. soldiers. A Panamanian journalist, Marshall Maclean, who witnessed the shooting was beaten and arrested.[30]

---

29. Quoted in *El Diario/La Prensa*, Oct. 9, 1990.
30. *The Washington Post*, Dec. 6, 1990.

Endara claimed that the unions that had participated in the job action had actually conspired with the police to overthrow the government. Within days, an executive order was passed into law which provided a cover for the most draconian assault on the rights of organized labor in Panama to date. Known as Law 25, it set the stage for the privatization campaign and the sell-off of the most productive and valuable assets of the Panamanian nation as demanded by the International Monetary Fund and USAID.

As the U.S. troops surrounded the police station in Curundú, one of the poorest neighborhoods in the capital, they were in turn surrounded by the residents of the area. Some threw stones. Others taunted the troops, jeering "Hussein, Hussein," a defiant reference to Sadam Hussein, in anticipation of the war then looming in the Gulf.

The working people of Panama have been the hardest hit by the sanctions, invasion and occupation. Panama's foreign debt is $6 billion. As described in our report, the top priority of the U.S.-installed government is paying off the banks and international lending institutions such as the IMF. This policy has had disastrous consequences for the workers in Panama.

On August 12, 1991 representatives of the Independent Commission of Inquiry interviewed Mauro Murrillo, the president of the National Council of Organized Labor in Panama (CONATO). His remarks summed up the present social, political and military situation in this beleaguered country.

"On the question of unemployment, an organization that compiles statistics on employment in Latin America and the Caribbean region calculates that now in Panama those who don't have a permanent job and those working only part-time, that is the under-employed, total some 40% of the labor force," said Murrillo.

"Those who can't find any work at all—who have to depend on a cousin, a brother or sister, their father or on their retired grandfather who is collecting a pension—now constitute 25% of the economically active population.

"The poverty rate here is alarming. Over the last 18 months [since the U.S. invasion] the poverty rate, as a percentage of the population, has exceeded that of Haiti. We are speaking of more than a million people living below poverty levels out of a population of 2.4 million people.

"But these figures aren't publicized because the mass media are controlled and manipulated in the interests of the present government. Despite a tremendous demand for the truth, one is unable to speak. The situation is very difficult.

"Panama is an occupied country. It is completely controlled, geographically, economically and politically... A powerful movement to fight for the interests of the workers from October to December last year mobilized more than 100,000 workers in the streets in energetic protests, demanding their rights.

"And the government brought out Law 25, passed last December... They were afraid that the strength of this movement would bring down their government. So they decided to use the excuse of the prison escape of Colonel Herrera and mix it all together.

"Despite the fact that the Attorney General himself said that one thing had absolutely nothing to do with the other, the workers were fired anyway. The Supreme Court decision on the workers' suit was very shrewd and was really a triumph for the government. It upheld the firing—the decapitation of the unions—of more than 500 leaders of the civil-service unions as well as some from the private sector...

"This is a government that acts using legal means against the interests of the people and of the workers. It is a government that calls itself 'democratic' but which is characterized by corruption, nepotism, injustice, arrogance. All this has shown itself during the last 18-19 months.

"So, we have become a country in which we are hostages in our own land. We say this because, before the Torrijos-Carter treaties, the courts and the judges and the governor in the Canal Zone were controlled by the United States If a crime were committed there, the accused would be tried by the U.S. authorities. However, after the Torrijos-Carter treaties this all disappeared—the courts, the judges, the legal jurisdiction.

"Now, however, with the signing of the Mutual Legal Assistance Treaty, U.S. judges can try Panamanians for alleged crimes committed in Panama without any problems. That is to say, we are no longer talking about U.S. legal jurisdiction over a small piece of our territory, but over the entire country.

"The United States is responsible for all this because it was the United States that imposed this government. So the people say, 'It is the Gringos' fault,' and 'Where are the millions of dollars in aid promised by the United Sttates?' The refugees of El Chorrillo are worse off now in the miserable substandard housing that was built for them. They were better off in the tenements they had before.

"So we come to the question of concerted action. This is a concept that we are learning through trial and error. We are trying to find a way to shift the balance of power in our favor. The workers here are trying to find a higher degree of unity regardless of political or ideological orientation. As far as the government is concerned, if CONATO, for example, holds a meeting, it is a conspiracy and must be dealt with...

"A year and one-half after the invasion and there is no freedom in Panama."

About South End Press

South End Press is a nonprofit, collectively run book publisher with over 150 titles in print. Since our founding in 1977, we have tried to meet the needs of readers who are exploring, or are already committed to, the politics of radical social change.

Our goal is to publish books that encourage critical thinking and constructive action on the key political, cultural, social, economic, and ecological issues shaping life in the United States and in the world. In this way, we hope to give expression to a wide diversity of democratic social movements and to provide an alternative to the products of corporate publishing.

If you would like a free catalog of South End Press books or information about our membership program—which offers two free books and a 40% discount on all titles—please write us at South End Press, 116 Saint Botolph Street, Boston, MA 02115.

Other titles of interest from South End Press:

The Sun Never Sets
Confronting the Network of Foreign Military Bases
edited by Joseph Gerson and Bruce Birchard

The Praetorian Guard
The U.S. in the New International Security State
John Stockwell

Freedom Under Fire: U.S. Civil Liberties in Times of War
Michael Linfield

Washington's War on Nicaragua
Holly Sklar

Necessary Illusions
Thought Control in Democratic Societies
Noam Chomsky

A Dream Compels Us
Voices of El Salvadoran Women
edited by New Americas Press